ARISE, AWAKE

ARISE, AWAKE

The inspiring stories of 10 young entrepreneurs who graduated from college into a business of their own

RASHMI BANSAL

BUSHFIRE PUBLISHERS

First published by Westland Ltd in 2015
Reprinted by Bushfire Publishers LLP in 2019
(Venture by Rashmi Bansal)
Core House, Off CG Road, Near Parimal Garden
Ahmedabad 380006

Bushfire and the Bushfire logo are the trademarks of Bushfire Publishers LLP, or its affiliates.

ISBN: 978-81931821-5-4

10 9 8 7 6 5 4 3 2 1

Content, page design and typesetting by JAM Venture Publishing Pvt. Ltd

Logo design by Surbhi Jain

Cover design by Idea Spice Design

Printed at Thomson Press (I) Ltd.

DEDICATED TO

My teacher, Sunil Handa
For the awakening in me

ACKNOWLEDGEMENTS

To all who have directly contributed to the making of this book.

My transcription team - Alekhya Rao, Shubham Singh, Abhijeet Yadav, Anchal Kumar, Priyanka (Writersmelon), Jyoti Arya and Sachin Whaval.

Saurav Roy of Idea Spice Design, for another crackling cover.

Pranay Gupta of 91 Springboard, for being a sounding board.

My partner, Niyati Patel, and my Man Friday, Ravish Kumar.

Aradhana Bisht, for her 'special touch' as editor.

Gautam Padmanabhan, my gentle and ever-cheerful publisher.

The sales team at Westland - KK, Rajaram and gang.

To all those near and dear to me.

This year has been a journey in solitude. A journey into my inner world.

I seek to harness the power of my mind.

To speak through intentions. To communicate without words.

My deep gratitude to all who have loved and supported me in this journey.

You know who you are. You are precious, you are part of my soul.

Arise ! Awake! And stop not
till the goal is reached.

– Swami Vivekananda

AUTHOR'S NOTE

I first wrote for a newspaper when I was 18 years old. It started out as a lark, a desire to see my name in print.

But when I sent my carefully typed article to the editor of *The Times of India*, all I received for my effort was a 'rejection slip'.

I tried again and again, and yet again. Each time I got the same impersonal response.

I should have got the message. That I am not 'good enough'. Instead, *mujhe aur josh aa gaya*. It became a sort of a game for me.

If I played long enough and hard enough, I could 'outwit the crocodile'.

One fine day, I opened the newspaper and there I saw it my name in print. I will never forget that moment. That feeling. That one-hundred-rupee cheque.

A journey of a thousand miles starts with a single step. But the road is slippery and wet. You don't have the right shoes. You don't have Google Maps.

Yet, you must put that foot forward.

You will stumble, you will fall. You will get up again, you will learn to walk.

Many will say – wait till you graduate. I say – why waste time? Right now you are free – to experiment, to walk on different paths.

Not just the path of mediocrity, well-travelled by others.

My college writing stint gave me clarity. At the end of my two years in IIM Ahmedabad, I opted out of placement.

I could do this because I knew 'what I am really good at'.

This is a secret embedded within you. A secret no one else can unlock.

Life is a massive multiplayer game, waiting for you to log on. So don your avatar, do your thing.

Many lives and many adventures await – your time starts now!

January 2015 ***Rashmi Bansal***
Mumbai

CONTENTS

RANKERS

They cracked the toughest entrance exams in the country. And then took on new challenges. Challenges for which there is no 'coaching class'.

CONTENTS

REPEATERS

The dudes who tried – and failed – but had the will to try again. Because nothing that is worth anything comes easily. And giving up is *not* an option.

REBELS WITH A CAUSE

These mavericks strayed away from the beaten path into weird and wonderful places. Because who you are is more than a 'placement'.

REBELS WITH A CAUSE

These mavericks strayed away from the beaten path into weird and wonderful places. Because who you are is more than a 'placement'.

P164 **HOLY RAVA MASALA**

Eshwar Vikas & Sudeep Sabat
(SRM Engineering College, Chennai)

DOSAMATIC

Born: Eshwar: 14 June 1991;

Sudeep Sabat: 19 April 1990

Two young engineers set out to create an automatic dosa machine. 3 years later, they have succeeded in producing the world's first tabletop 'dosa printer' and secured orders from 100 restaurant owners.

CONTENTS

RANKERS

They cracked the toughest entrance exams in the country. And then took on new challenges. Challenges for which there is no 'coaching class'.

Abhinav Lal & Shashank N D (right)

LIFE IS A BEACH

Shashank N D & Abhinav Lal
(NIT Surathkal)
PRACTO TECHNOLOGIES

It was the tenth out of the 10 ideas they had to start a new business, and it clicked. This startup, born in the final year of college, is now a ₹20 crore company, serving 10,000 doctors across India.

On my first day at IIM Ahmedabad, I found a highly intelligent but equally eccentric guy seated next to me.

"Where are you from?" I asked.

"NIT Surathkal." Perhaps seeking to impress, he added, "The only college in India with its own private beach."

Truth be told, I was impressed. Years later, when I visited the campus, I physically verified this fact.

I can also verify the fact that NIT Surathkal continues to produce intelligent eccentrics like Shashank N D and Abhinav Lal.

"Back in 2005, when we joined college, nobody had heard of the term 'entrepreneurship'. NIT-K was one of the first colleges in India to start an E-Cell."

As Shashank and Abhinav worked to spread awareness about entrepreneurship, a strange thing happened. The e-virus entered their system and they decided to start a company themselves.

This venture, started in the fourth year of college, has blossomed and grown into Practo - a software being used by 10,000 doctors. A company which employs over 300 people with revenues close to ₹20 crore.

Today, NIT-K is still the only college with a private beach but hundreds of colleges have E-Cells. To these colleges, I throw a challenge: Can each E-Cell inspire 10 students to start a small business while they are still on campus?

Here's to the intelligent eccentrics of the world - may their tribe increase!

LIFE IS A BEACH

Shashank N D & Abhinav Lal
(NIT Surathkal)
PRACTO TECHNOLOGIES

Shashank N D was born and brought up in Bangalore in a standard middle class family.

"My parents were both in government jobs. My father was with Visvesvaraya Iron and Steel Plant (VISL), while my mother was working in Bharat Electronics Ltd (BEL)."

It was a joint family, a big family but nobody in the field of business. Shashank attended the National Public School, Bangalore, from KG, right up to Class 12. He was an average student - more into extracurricular activities and sports.

"I was flowing with the wind, with no inspiration whatsoever to do anything. But in Class 12, it suddenly hit me."

While friends and classmates were busy preparing for various entrance exams and knew what they wanted to do in life - he didn't have a clue. One evening, Shashank mentioned to his parents that some of his friends had qualified for the National Olympiad in mathematics and science.

"I saw this poster in my dorm for E-Cell. At that time I had no idea what entrepreneurship was... I didn't even know what it meant."

"Why haven't you tried?" they asked.

Baat chubh gayi. Shashank got up from the dining table, called up a friend and bugged him about when was the next qualifying test. And, basically, he decided to 'get serious'.

"I pretty much locked myself in one room for the whole year, grew a huge beard and did my entire education in that year!"

Not only did Shashank qualify for the Informatic Olympiad, he went a step further. When the AIEEE (All India Engineering Entrance Examination) results were declared – to everyone's surprise – the once happy-go-lucky student had made it to the prestigious NIT-K (Surathkal).

"Surathkal basically changed my life. The peer group was amazing, so was the standard of competition. You had people from all over the country!"

Shashank joined NIT-K in July 2005. In September 2006, he heard of the term 'entrepreneurship' for the very first time. A senior in college – Ayush Jhunjhunwala – had returned from an internship in the US. At Stanford University, he was exposed to the idea of 'E-Cell' (Entrepreneurship Cell) and decided to set up a similar club on the NIT campus.

"I saw a poster in my dorm for 'Eforea' and it seemed like a very new and exciting thing."

The introductory talk cast a spell on Shashank and he immediately signed up for the club. While many applied, only 4 second-year students were selected. One of them was Abhinav Lal – from the same branch and same hostel as Shashank. Little did they know what lay ahead!

At Eforea, the first task was to generate awareness about entrepreneurship. To do that, the young engineers had to first educate themselves. The Eforea gang travelled to ISB Hyderabad and then landed up at IIT Bombay for 'Eureka'.

"I remember, we were all sleeping because the discussion was very boring... then this guy from rediff.com, called Ajit Balakrishnan, comes and the stage lights up!"

The majority of speakers were from large companies like Microsoft – Ajit was an entrepreneur. He spoke with enthusiasm, with energy and passion and that's what connected with the young audience.

Shashank thought to himself, "Wow! I want to be like that guy."

The Eforea team now had a simple strategy – attend only those sessions where the founder of the company is speaking. *Those* are the guys to learn from!

"We returned to campus, eager to start sharing all we had seen and heard!"

Thus, Eforea organised a series of events – talks by entrepreneurs, panel discussions and so on. Getting speakers to Surathkal was not easy but the students were persistent. One of the many people they reached out to was Patrick Turner – a professor of entrepreneurship at INSEAD Business School. Not only did he accept but he also came down at his own expense.

"There was a tremendous buzz on campus... the whole auditorium was full!"

Professor Turner's message was simple: "You can invent, you can lead, put in the hard work and you can make anything happen."

"We travelled to different places at our own expense to understand 'what is entrepreneurship'... and that changed my life for ever."

"The whole third year was frustrating - we had many ideas but no results to show. In our final year of college is when it all clicked."

The goal of life is not campus placement, you can create your own path. What's more, there is a science behind it.

"By the end of the talk, we all understood that 'entrepreneur' is not a dirty word, it's something exciting!"

Over the course of the year, Eforea organised many more such events and membership exploded. At the end of the second year, Shashank became the club coordinator. Under his tenure, Eforea organised 'Ignition', the first entrepreneurship summit for colleges in south India. It was a huge success. But somewhere, there was this itch to do more, to actually get a taste of running your own business.

"In our third year, we did a bunch of things... tried out different ideas."

Shashank took up a project for Tavant Technologies, a company where a senior from NIT-K was working. Tavant had launched a product called 'SocialWay' which they wanted to popularise in colleges.

"We put up posters, motivated people to sign up but it never really took off. Nonetheless, we were so involved that it felt like our own venture!"

The young team used to go to the Tavant office in Bangalore, sit there and brainstorm on 'what to do'. They spent nights together, dreaming about a business and came up with the idea of a social network for colleges.

"The very next day, we read a report in the newspaper about somebody who's already done that* and got funded $10 million!"

Another day, another new idea... It was around this time

---

* The company was Minglebox.com, funded by Sequoia capital.

that Abhinav and Shashank worked together to build the club website.

"College brings together all kinds of people... when you hang out with each other, you find someone with whom you just click."

And that's exactly what happened. While both were IT students, Abhinav was more the coder while Shashank had a fine marketing brain. Together, they dreamed up numerous web-based ventures - from a stock market program to software for marriage halls. And it was all one grand adventure.

"We used to come to Bangalore on our own expense, put on a suit and attend networking events. We would talk like we are already these big shots who know everything but actually we went to learn!"

And what did their parents have to say about all this? Nothing - because they had no clue.

At the end of the third year of college, Abhinav and Shashank decided it was now or never. The tenth out of the 10 ideas they'd come up with was a software for doctors. This time, they would do it properly, seriously.

"We registered this company called Practo Technologies in 2008. I borrowed ₹10,000 from my mother, printed visiting cards and we started approaching doctors."

The modus operandi was to open the yellow pages and call up random doctors, saying, "Hello doctor, we have designed a software just for you! When can you meet us?"

In truth, there was no software - it was just a basic concept and a PPT with a few slides. Ever the optimist,

"We recycled so many different ideas, so many different things that we finally came down to the last idea on our list - 'approach doctors to sell something'."

"This idea made sense because it was big and it would easily take us a long time to accomplish – that's what made it exciting!"

Shashank decided to organise an event where they would bring together 25 doctors and make a presentation. The venue was a hospital and Shashank's mother pitched in by organising some juice and chips. But things didn't go as planned.

"It was the worst event of my entire life!" recalls Shashank. "My suit didn't fit properly, the pitch went badly and the audience showed no interest..."

In fact, most of the doctors said it was a terrible idea – 'don't disturb me again'.

"We were just destroyed after that... We'd spent all our money and exhausted all our ideas."

It looked like the end of the road...

Then, one doctor – Dr Mohammed Ali – came back and said, "I like your idea – when can you meet me?"

He was a young chap and probably the least important among all the doctors who had attended. By this time, Shashank and Abhinav had practically given up and were in no mood to respond.

"He was the one who made 5-6 calls and persuaded us to meet him!"

At his clinic, Dr Ali explained the problem. Patients were supposed to come for check-ups at regular intervals. But they had to be reminded. Could this reminder be automated?

It didn't sound like a very big or interesting problem to solve but the client was willing to pay.

"In fact, he wrote us a cheque of ₹5000 on the spot." It was the very first payment received by Practo Technologies.

"We came back and said – what to do now? This guy has already paid us so now we have to build it!"

The third year had just ended and there was a long vacation. Shashank's parents happened to own a house which was lying unused, locked up for the last 8 years. There was no furniture, no appliances, just a working tap and an electricity connection. Just the kind of place two young men could work in peace, under the influence of *achaar* and *aalu parathas*.

"Abhinav did not go home that summer, he stayed back in Bangalore and we wrote code non-stop for two weeks. At the end of it, we had a working prototype."

The software had just 4-5 basic features such as storing patient names and sending SMS reminders. But when Dr Ali started using it, he couldn't stop raving about it.

"The feedback we got was so good, we started thinking, okay, there may be something in this!"

Around the same time, Shashank's father was undergoing a knee operation. His reports had to be taken to an eminent doctor for a second opinion. The file was in a hard-copy format so Shashank had to use his Sony Ericsson P1 camera phone to photograph every page. These pictures were then downloaded to a computer and emailed to the concerned doctor.

"I really could not understand why the hospital which was charging us lakhs for the surgery could not provide reports in digital format!"

In fact, all medical records are clumsily stored in a file, from the time of 'first vaccination'. It's a good, loving

"No one had ever heard of a kid starting a company in college, continuing with it and making something great. At least not in India."

"Internally, we had said that we'll wrap this up in 3 to 6 months. *Jab tak chalega chalega*. But then we started enjoying it."

feeling to see the trouble your parents have taken but then you wonder - what if it ever got lost? A Big Idea started forming at the back of Shashank's mind - the idea that each and every patient can and must have his or her healthcare record online.

"This was the vision forming in my head but, in the meantime, we could see money coming in from doctors by solving their immediate problems."

In fact, Dr Ali was so happy with the Practo software, he readily gave references to several of his friends. Soon the young engineers had more than 10 clients willing to cough up ₹5000–10,000 each.

"We got a lot of feedback from the doctors and we kept working on our product... In fact, we stayed back in Bangalore and never went back to college!"

Abhinav's family in distant Bihar had no clue about this, while Shashank told his parents that, with projects and placements going on, there were no classes. What's more, he convinced them to invest a lakh of rupees into the company.

"They saw how excited I was, so full of confidence and doing something. So they were more than happy to encourage and support me."

Of course, they thought it was a passing phase and that, eventually, better sense would prevail. Meanwhile, the boys were having the time of their life. They continued to live in the spare house, partying hard during the day and coding late into the night. Lunch and dinner were usually takeaways, using 'pocket money' sent by parents.

"We had no responsibilities whatsoever... we spent on good food and what was left went into the business!"

The business was both 'serious' and non-serious - at the same time. While they loved the work they were doing, the future was uncertain. Then there was the lure of campus placement. Hailing from a very small town called Devgad in Bihar, it was expected of Abhinav to study hard, get into IIT or NIT and, ultimately, go for a 'good job'.

"I told Shashank that I need to go to campus and take a placement, otherwise my mom will get suspicious."

So the day after college opened, Abhinav landed up in Surathkal and applied to a random company which was hiring. That company happened to be Satyam.

"I called up my mom and said - I got a job. So like, okay - that's done."

Now Shashank started feeling the heat. Every other night, friends would call up to share 'breaking news' on campus. How so and so guy got into Microsoft with a package of ₹12 lakh p.a., how they were all busy partying in the hostel.

"Sitting in Bangalore, with an unknown future, I began to feel insecure."

After 4 months, Shashank couldn't bear it. He went to Surathkal and decided to sit for interviews. As luck would have it, the very first company he tried for gave him an offer letter. Mission accomplished, the same night Shashank took the bus back to Bangalore.

So what did they actually do that entire year?

"We were basically discovering things - small, small things. Now I realise that we spent the whole year doing so little, but at that time it felt very good."

I am not a coding whiz, it's just that if there is a problem in front of me, I have to solve it... does not matter what time or how much work it takes!"

"From Day 1, our hardcore philosophy has been – you can't just have a good product, you have to be good at sales."

The 'things to do' included meeting doctors, making sales pitches, tweaking and updating the software. As well as attending conferences and networking events. Every time they were introduced as 'student entrepreneurs', there was a moment of stunned silence.

"It gave us a real high to know we are the youngest guys in any room!"

The year was 2008 and the buzz around the internet was growing. Sites like Facebook were gaining popularity; Flipkart was a small startup selling books. But there was a sense *ki kuchch ho raha hai* (something is happening).

With each month, the challenges increased and so did the involvement. Each time they closed a new customer or deployed a new piece of code, there was the high of achievement. People are using something *you* have created and it's making a difference.

By February 2009, there was an improved version of Practo, version 2.0. The company now had 20-25 clients and continued to get very positive feedback.

"That gave us a lot of confidence and we said, let's go all in!"

A client mentioned that there was an exhibition happening at the Palace Grounds in Bangalore. A very big event where all the dentists in the city would be participating. It was the month of May, just one month before graduation – a 'now or never' moment.

"We took the last ₹1 lakh in our bank account and spent the entire money at the conference."

While the stall itself cost ₹60,000, flex banners and brochures were another ₹30,000. But the effort paid off.

On the very first day, the Practo stall attracted a large number of people. So much so, that there was no place to stand inside.

"We actually had to call our friends and say - please come here to help out!"

Visitors were fascinated by the demo. When an appointment was added and the doctor's cellphone beeped, his face lit up. This was the 'aha' moment for Abhinav, the moment he realised, "I want to take this forward!"

By this time, Abhinav had landed an even better job than Satyam - he had an offer from ZS Software with a package of ₹11 lakh. Which made it all the more difficult.

"When I went back home and said I am not taking up this job, everyone said I was crazy."

But he managed to convince his mom by making a deal.

"Let me do this for a year and if Practo doesn't take off, I will go back and get a job!"

Meanwhile, Shashank faced the same dilemma. A package of ₹7 lakh per annum wasn't something to turn your back on, that too in the year 2009. The market had crashed and jobs were scarce, only a fool would give up a good placement.

"When everyone said the same thing, I thought - it will be good to prove them wrong!"

Thus, the two 22-year-olds decided to follow their foolish hearts. Exams cleared, degree in hand - it was back to business. But now came the reality check. Student-life had ended, this was no longer a hobby, or a nice way to show off.

"As a 'student entrepreneur', you can be average and still get noticed. Now you are like everyone else - there's no excuse for not being the best!"

The end of college also meant the end of pocket money. You are officially an adult and have to fend for yourself.

"The good thing is that it made us a lot more serious - I would say that was the actual birth of the company!"

"To sell something, you need to create 'magic' – when it's magic, you will have a cheque in your hands in 5 minutes."

The late-night parties, movie marathons and Dominos deliveries stopped. The crunching and coding started in earnest. There were also some serious conversations about investing in the business. Thus far, it was Shashank who had put in approximately ₹5 lakh. Now Abhinav wanted to contribute as well.

"Between the two of us, we pooled in ₹10-12 lakh."

This money was essentially needed to build a team. The first people they approached were NIT Surathkal batchmates.

"We said, 'Hey – we have this great idea, why don't you join us'!"

Siddharth Nihalani was the first to come on board. A brilliant guy, willing to give up a secure job to work for this unknown company – simply because he wanted to be 'different'. Within two months, 4 others had joined Practo – two were coders while the rest were in sales.

The initial team received modest salaries of ₹10-15,000 per month. But there was one big perk of working at Practo – free accommodation. The boys continued to make use of Shashank's empty house. The ground floor served as the 'office', while the first floor was the 'dorm'.

"We used to tell folks – all you gotta do is get your own mattress!"

The boys also picked up computers at throwaway prices from friends who were going to the US for higher studies.

"We used to do rupee to rupee accounting, yet money was always tight. It's like you're constantly under pressure!"

The only way out was to increase sales. There was no definite plan, just a belief that if you try hard enough – you will succeed. Shashank sent one of his team members to Chennai and another to Mumbai.

"Don't come back – stay there and sell as much as you can!" was the simple directive.

There was no budget for a hotel – the trick was to find a friend working in Mumbai and stay with him for a few days. Before moving on to the next friend's house. The office was a table at Café Coffee Day and a mobile phone.

The first 6 months was do, die and *jugaad*. After that, orders started coming in – 10, 15, 20 orders a month. The turnover was between ₹1–2 lakh, in a good month it went as high as ₹4 lakh.

"We started breaking even – at least we could make ends meet."

Through this period of struggle, there was one guiding light. Morpheus Venture partners* had just launched an accelerator program for very early-stage startups. The website stated, 'we are going to help entrepreneurs who want to make it big' – which sounded extremely attractive.

"We applied and after speaking to us for 15 minutes, the partners said, 'We like you, come on board'!"

The deal was simple: each startup would receive mentoring, advice and business connections. In return, Morpheus received a 4–8% equity stake. Other companies in this first accelerator batch included Interviewstreet and Commonfloor.

"We didn't get any money but just the fact that *someone* believes in you made us feel better."

Morpheus was also able to provide valuable inputs on the sales and marketing side. Sameer Guglani, Indus Khaitan and Nandini Hirianniah were experienced entrepreneurs – their presence at important meetings added a lot of credibility to the Practo sales pitch.

---

* Morpheus Ventures was India's first private startup accelerator. It shut down in Feb 2014.

"We know we can't do everything, we don't intend to do everything, but we can solve one problem at a time."

"They looked older and had 'venture partners' on their business card. So clients took us more seriously."

But at the end of the day, a sales deal is closed by a good salesman. The Practo team quickly learnt the tricks of the trade and the most valuable trick of all was 'instant gratification'. If you capture the doctor's imagination, solve his problem in front of his eyes – you will get the business.

"You have to create magic and you have just 5 minutes to do it. If it's not magic, he will take 6 months to buy it. If it's magic, you walk out with the cheque."

Luckily, Practo lent itself to 'magic' quite easily. The doctor would be asked to input his name and number into the software and suddenly his mobile would vibrate.

"Why don't you use this to send reminders to patients," the sales guy would say.

"Wow – I never knew that was possible!" the doctor would say and happily sign up.

The decision was made easier by the offer of a 30-day 'free trial' period. After that, they would pay an annual fee. This was quite revolutionary at the time.

"The Software As A Service (SAAS) concept was unheard of in India. We were one of the first companies to offer it!"

Doctors were used to buying a software for ₹5000 and installing it on their PCs. Now, they were being asked to pay ₹10,000 – every year – to use Practo. So, while they loved the product, getting them to pay that premium was the tough part. Both a science and an art.

The scientific part was the 'dashboard' at the back end, where you could see which doctor was logging in and actually using the software. These doctors were more willing to pay up. The 'art' was building a connection with the doctor at a human level. Partly, this was through references from other doctors. But it often went beyond that.

"You go with the doctor to pick up his daughter; you go with the doctor to eat his lunch... you build a relationship."

By March 2010, Practo had achieved a respectable sales turnover of ₹20 lakh and started approaching investors. But there was no interest whatsoever. It was a bad time to raise capital and, to make matters worse, Practo was targeting the Indian market.

"The VCs saw a team of 22-year-olds selling software to Indians, that too doctors. It was an unproven model - nobody even wanted to entertain us!"

When the world rejects you, there are two options. Change and become what the world wants - or stay true to yourself. The chameleon blends in - never stands out.

"What kept us going was the response from doctors, we were solving a genuine problem - so there were no doubts."

Persistence pays. In September 2010, Shailendra Singh of Sequoia Capital agreed to meet with Practo. The young team was excited - it was a 'red carpet' moment.

"I remember, we had gone for a sales meeting and in Bombay, you use local train, right? So I made sure I came back, got ready - because you don't want to smell bad for this meeting - and took a taxi which was quite an expensive thing at that time!"

The Sequoia office in Parel is lined with photographs of super-successful internet entrepreneurs - from Steve Jobs to Sergey Brin and Larry Page. Sequoia was an early investor in both Apple and Google. Shashank quickly started taking photos.

"I started sending pics to everybody, saying - see I am in this office! Because honestly, I thought I will never be coming back here again."

Then Shailendra Singh walked in and what followed was an

amazing one-hour session. Very different from any other session with a prospective investor.

"Usually, a VC will ask you - 'How big is this going to be?' 'Why is the market segment so small? 'Why haven't you used terms like ROI in your presentation?'"

Instead of all that, Shailendra Singh simply asked, "Why are you doing this?"

That set the whole meeting on fire. Shashank explained that Practo was more than a software for doctors - there was a bigger vision and mission. To digitise all medical records of patients.

Shashank spoke freely, frankly and passionately. At the end of one hour, Shailendra said, "Sounds like a fair idea - we will give you this much (money)."

The young man could not believe his ears.

"At that time, we had a 4-digit number in the bank and then he said, we will give you some 8-digit figure. Surely, he must be joking!"

Still in shock, Shashank called Morpheus Venture partners and narrated what just happened. They, too, were speechless - no company in their portfolio had received an on-the-spot offer.

Morpheus called the investor to reconfirm.

Shailendra said, "It's a great team, great product, great market and nobody has discovered them - so, yes, I am ready to back them!"

The deal took 6 months to close - during that time, Practo continued to operate frugally and ever on the brink.

"We had an HDFC account, I used to operate it, we had to literally wait for a payment to come and then clear another payment."

This *chindi* phase ended when the Sequoia money actually came into Practo in March 2011. The visible fallout was better salaries, better food, better beer. But as far as work went, the team was pushing even harder.

Because the Sequoia deal wasn't just about money, it was about a sense of validation.

"One year before, your parents and everyone else says you are a fool for doing this. Now this VC, which has supported great companies, is saying – maybe you have it in you! You feel like the 'king of the world!'"

The trick is to not sit on that imaginary throne for too long, but to go out and conquer new kingdoms. To do this, you need more generals and more foot soldiers.

"Our focus was on sales, we had to increase the revenues and make sure we got the next round of funding."

The sales team quickly expanded with the help of a naukri.com database and HR consultants. As the team grew, a 'proper' office was needed in different cities. All this cost money – which happened to be in the bank – but was difficult to spend.

"We used to have a small table-and-chair kind of space under a staircase in Sitladevi Road, Mahim, and we paid ₹5000 for that. That was how careful we were with money!"

Before signing the lease for a new office in Mumbai, Shashank called one of his board members and asked, "Is it okay if we spend ₹35,000 per month on rent?"

He said, "Go ahead – you need it. And don't ever call me for something like this again!"

Yet, it was the Protestant work ethic, which kept Practo alive before the money came in, which helped it thrive after. The business 'grew like crazy' in just 6 months. From a couple of lakhs a month, the revenues shot up to tens of lakhs. By the year ending March 2012, Practo's turnover was close to ₹2 crore with 25 employees and 6 sales offices.

That's when Sequoia came back and said, "We like what you did with small money, we want to give you more money."

In mid-2012, Sequoia invested $4.6 million (₹25 crore) in Practo. The first thing the team decided to do with the money was build a website to empower patients. Launched in August 2012, practo.com allows you to find out where a doctor is available and book an appointment.

In October 2012, Practo expanded to Singapore and, 3 months later, opened an office there.

"We know India is a very big market but somewhere there is an ambition to be on a global healthcare platform."

The overseas office also serves a strategic objective - Practo is now a Singaporean company with an Indian subsidiary. This will make it easier for the company to have an IPO.

"Sequoia has a long-term view but at some point any investor needs an exit!"

An entrepreneur is always looking for growth, raring to try out a dozen ideas. A good VC provides a nudge in the right direction.

"At one point, we wanted to enter B2B e-commerce but Sequoia told us that's a tough space - chances of success are low. Ultimately, we decided against it."

The focus remains on doctors and patients, with the Practo software adding many new and useful features. Doctors can now send prescriptions via email or sms, maintain clinical notes, test results and X-rays. The software also takes care of billing and inventory, and helps clinics deal with patients. For example, the telephone lines at many clinics are continuously busy.

"We offer a 'virtual receptionist' service called Practo Hello which allows you to book an appointment 24X7."

The team is also excited about introducing a tablet specifically for doctors. The idea is to allow patients to use Practo software instead of filling up cumbersome forms.

In the last two years, Practo has grown rapidly, with over 300 employees and estimated revenues of ₹20 crore. 10,000 doctors actively use the software, while over one lakh medical practitioners are registered on the practo.com website.

"Our goal in the next 2-3 years is to reach 60-70% of all doctors in India and be in 4-5 countries."

The surprising thing is that the same problems exist everywhere. Whether you are in India or Dubai, you don't know the average waiting time at a clinic or which doctor patients are happy with. That kind of information will soon be available on practo.com.

"Unlike banking, penetration of technology in healthcare is low. That's our biggest challenge and biggest opportunity!"

Which is why all the 7 initial team members are still with Practo. Holding shares in the company and important roles in the organisation.

"Everyone has grown together and that's a great feeling! We never wanted folks to feel we are the only two entrepreneurs – it's an entrepreneurial team."

For life is like a game of football – the team that passes the ball, scores the goal.

Play for love, play for money, play to win! The ball is right there – in front of you.

ADVICE TO YOUNG ENTREPRENEURS

Abhinav

It's good to start early. Starting a business in college is the best way to use your time. You have no responsibility, you have nothing to lose. Now the question is - once you graduate, should you take a job or continue your business? My mindset was - I am going to first work for a couple of years, but the decision of just jumping into it and riding the wave was the best thing that I could possibly have done.

The second thing is - it's really important to stick to your vision. The vision should not be, "I want a ₹100 crore company", but, "I am going to solve this problem." When you are solving a problem, everything else automatically falls into place.

Shashank

There have been great companies that have come out from India, the chances of success have increased. So there's even more reason to jump in and build something truly magnificent!

Secondly, ambition is good to have, everyone wants to be rich and famous but it does not happen overnight. Don't fall in the trap of going to too many networking events to talk about your idea, instead work on the idea.

You are a 21- or 22- year-old and have a lot of things to prove. Things will not come easy to you. Work really hard, build a great product and sell, sell, sell!

In India, if you want a successful company, you have to give at least 75% of your time to sales. When I say sales, I mean 'face to face' meetings. Look at Justdial, Naukri or Zomato - they have all made money through feet on street.

Stay grounded and stay focused, automatically, success will come to you.

Puneet Mittal

Sourabh Bansal

Sidharth Bansal

YOU CAN DO MAGIC

Sourabh Bansal (IIT Kharagpur), Puneet Mittal (CA) & Sidharth Bansal (IIT Delhi, IIM Lucknow)

MAGICRETE

In the year 2008, a fresh graduate from IIT Kharagpur and a fresh chartered accountant decided to shake up an age-old industry. Today, Magicrete is a ₹150 crore company which is changing the face of construction across the country.

IIT Kharagpur is the IIT in the 'middle of nowhere'. Kharagpur is a sleepy little town with the world's longest railway platform - but it has no mall, no multiplex, not even a half-decent restaurant.

When I first visited IIT KGP in the year 2008, I thought to myself, "How quaint!"

The best way to spend a long night on the campus is hanging out with friends. Sitting in someone's room, chattering about everything under the sun. Having a '*bhaat* session'.

In one such hostel room - D-206, R K Hall of Residence - Sourabh Bansal was cooking some *khichdi*. Not with dal and rice, but with some crazy ideas. The topic was, 'what do you want to do in life?' *Koi kuch keh raha tha, koi kuch aur*. When suddenly, the aforementioned young man stood up and wrote a number on the wall - '5000 crore'.

"I said, I want to start a business and I will take it to ₹5000 crore."

At that time, Sourabh was a third-year student. He did not have a business card that read, 'Founder of XYZ Campus Startup'. But he knew *ki kuch apna karna hai.*

At placement time, the startups folded up - few could resist the lure of a job. But Sourabh did. There was no concrete plan but he knew *koi na koi* business *pakad lenge.* After all, he was from Surat - a city of entrepreneurs.

"Then there was this misplaced confidence that if others can do it, with my IIT degree, I can do it better!"

7 years later, he has proven just that. His company, Magicrete, has crossed a turnover of ₹150 crore and is a leader in its field. But there is still a long way to go.

The walls of D-206 may have been repainted but those magic figures are stuck in Sourabh Bansal's mind.

"*Ek din karenge, zaroor karenge! 5000 crore!!*"

Every room has 4 walls. All it needs is someone to get up and scribble a dream on one of them.

And believe in that dream, live that dream, continue to dream - with eyes wide open.

YOU CAN DO MAGIC

Sourabh Bansal (IIT Kharagpur), Puneet Mittal (CA) & Sidharth Bansal (IIT Delhi, IIM Lucknow) MAGICRETE

"My father was a director (exports) with a textile firm. In 1998, he became an entrepreneur when he got into quicklime manufacturing."

At that time, Sourabh was a student of Class 10 and started helping out. He would tag along for client visits, monitor the factory when daddy was away, and prepare marketing materials along with younger brother, Sidharth.

Sourabh soon started feeling, "I want to start my own business." Although commerce was the logical choice, his father had a different line of thinking.

He said, "*Aage jaakar* technocrats *ka* time *hai* – you must take up technology as a subject."

In any case, 'good students' are generally herded into science. Thus, Sourabh joined the famous Bansal Classes at Kota, for IIT JEE coaching. And made it to IIT Kharagpur. With a rank of 1700+, he didn't get into the 4-year BTech course, hence opted for a 5-year dual degree (Industrial Engineering and Management).

"Tenth standard *mein ekdum bhed-chaal jaisa hota hai* (In the tenth standard, I just followed the herd). I followed my friends into engineering."

"First two years I was in a state of euphoria *ki* IIT *mein* admission *ho gaya, ab toh* everything will come easily in life."

By third year, Sourabh realised that there is a long journey ahead. Choices to be made, *aage kya karna hai.* Everybody was smart, and very competitive. Some were preparing for GRE, others for CAT. But Sourabh had no interest in further studies - he did *not* want to spend two more years in a classroom. *Bahut padhai ho gayi* - time to go out there and *do* something in the real world!

"Actually, we had courses like supply chain and entrepreneurship in the dual-degree course itself. I wouldn't say it was same as what you get from an MBA college, but the basics were covered."

A good student but never strong in calculus, Sourabh was a 6 pointer on campus. This ruled out the possibility of getting a 'fundu' placement. But Sourabh had no inclination towards a job, in any case. His mind was brimming with ideas; the question was *which* idea would make for a good business.

"I had done my BTech project on RFID, so my first thought was something related to that. Another idea I considered was an online road-freight marketplace. A third one was starting a digital ad network."

Like that - *yeh bhi, woh bhi,* many exciting ideas! Most of them had *something* to do with organising the unorganised sector. Sourabh used these ideas to enter business-plan and strategy competitions at various techno-management fests. At IIT Chennai, one such plan stood third in the annual Social Business Plan competition.

"The plan was to help tsunami-affected fishermen through GPS-assisted boats."

While Sourabh was wrestling with the dilemma of 'what to do?', his brother, Sidharth, was on a different path. A year younger to Sourabh, he was the 'brilliant' one who was always at the top of his class. Sidharth was pursuing Engineering Physics at IIT Delhi and would graduate the same year. But he had taken the CAT exam and hoped to join a consulting firm.

"Somewhere we thought it's good for one of us to take a more conventional route. And join the business later, once it grows big enough!"

Woh to sab baad ki baat hai, for now – the time to leave IIT Kharagpur was drawing near. And Sourabh still had no clear direction.

A couple of months before graduating, his dad's friend in Surat mentioned 'solar power' as an emerging area. Sourabh began reading about it and discovered there was a lot of buzz around a technology called 'thin film solar'. The young man returned to Surat in May 2007, all set to work on this idea.

"It seemed to be a good opportunity and uncle was ready to invest in the project as well."

Sourabh spent 3 months researching the business and even went to Germany to attend some exhibitions. He soon realised that, in Europe, solar power is heavily subsidised by the government – hence companies are profitable. India did not have any such incentive.

"Ultimately, we dropped the idea and I started working with my dad in lime manufacturing."

"*Mujhe kabhi woh* charm *nahin tha ki* job *mein jaana hai*, I never felt *ki* I wanted to work for someone else."

"Dream big, ideate *karo*, there are people with funds, funds is never a challenge."

When a new brain enters an old business, it gets a shot of adrenaline. Sourabh started thinking about how to make the factory more efficient and how to scale up production. But who would buy the extra output?

"The main use for quicklime is effluent treatment. I started thinking *ki* lime *ka aur kya kiya ja sakta hai,* what can be the forward integration?"

One morning, Sourabh noticed that a customer had placed a very large order - not the usual 50-100 tons, but thousands of tons, of lime. His curiosity was piqued - *yeh log itne* lime *ka karenge kya*? The company was called Siporex and Sourabh discovered they were manufacturing 'Autoclaved Aerated Concrete (AAC) blocks.'

"I decided to go and see their factory, to understand what they are doing exactly."

Sourabh made a trip to Pune and acted as if he wanted to be a distributor for their products. He was shown around the plant and he quickly concluded - there is a lot of scope in this industry. The question which bothered him, however, was why aren't there more companies in this line of business? At that time, apart from Siporex, there were only 3 other manufacturers of AAC blocks in the entire country.

"When I researched the product, I found that AAC blocks are 10 times the size of normal bricks but 70% lighter in weight. However, they were not used widely because the cost was 2X."

If the cost could be brought down, there was a huge potential market. Of course, it was a capital-intensive project - setting up a single factory would cost at least ₹25 crore. Where would a fresh graduate get this kind of money?

"I always had this thing in my head that I don't want to take a single rupee from my dad. Besides, his business was not so big that he could make such an investment."

But somewhere in his heart Sourabh knew *ki 'paisa aa jayega'*. A good idea is like a magnet, which will attract the right investor.

The young engineer studied the market - and he was excited! Brick manufacturing is a ₹50,000 crore industry but unlike steel or cement, there were no organised players. No well-known brand. No consistent quality.

"I thought that when there are listed companies in steel and cement, why not in bricks?"

Sourabh also looked at what had happened in Europe, what had happened in Asia and concluded that India would follow the global trend. In China, 50% of the buildings were being constructed with AAC blocks. Armed with this knowledge, he prepared a concrete business plan. With a more efficient operation, lower cost of production.

"The Siporex factory was using a diesel boiler, whereas coal boilers are 60-70% cheaper. Like that, there were many areas where I knew we can bring the cost down."

The cost of AAC blocks would still be 20-50% higher than brick but the builder would save on mortar, plaster and steel. Hence, the overall cost of construction would be much lower. It was an attractive proposition, ready to roll out to investors.

By this time, Sidharth was a second-year student of IIM Lucknow. He had just completed his summer internship with Baring Private Equity. Using his contacts, Sidharth arranged a meeting with the senior managers. The Bansal

"Initially, I wanted to retain a majority stake but then I became practical."

> ***Jo bahut zyada ginti karne wala hoga shayad isme* enter *hi nahi ho paata...* (The one who only adds up numbers cannot enter such a field).”**

brothers presented a bold business plan which projected a turnover of ₹1000 crore with 10 plants, in 5 years' time.

“Looking back, our plan was too ambitious. We were young and full of *josh*, we did not know the challenges we would have to face!”

Nevertheless, Baring 'liked the idea'. But as a growth capital fund, which typically invests $5 million or more in established companies, they declined to invest.

“They said, 'You are a startup. We do not invest in startups.' So then I started approaching angel investors.”

In the city of Surat, angels come in the form of 'uncles' - people known to your family who are HNIs (High Net Worth Individuals). One such uncle was Mr Rajesh Poddar. A sound businessman, Mr Poddar studied the project closely - and found it promising. What's more, he was convinced that Sourabh was the right person to lead the project. Young *hai, lekin dum hai.*

Rajesh Poddar agreed to invest ₹10 crore in return for a 70% equity stake.

“I was initially hesitant as I had to part with a majority stake in the company. But then I thought, I am just starting my career, *mujh par kisi ne itna* trust *kiya hai* - let me do it!”

Once the deal was struck, Puneet Mittal came into the picture. At that time, Puneet was a CA student, waiting to appear for his final exams. Puneet's father and Rajesh Poddar were partners in a textile unit. So there was a deep sense of trust between the two families.

“Mr Poddar asked me to take a look at this new business and see if I would like to join it.”

Puneet applied his accounting fundas to the project plan and concluded that the numbers added up. But anything can add up on paper, ultimately it's a leap of faith.

"Gut feeling *wali baat thi ki bhai* risk *toh hai, par mehnat karenge toh ho jayega*. (My gut feel was that there is an element of risk but if we work hard, we will be able to do it.)"

In April 2008, Magicrete Building Solutions Pvt Ltd was incorporated as a company with Rajesh Poddar, Sourabh Bansal and Puneet Mittal on the board of directors. Sourabh was designated CEO, while Puneet took the mantle of CFO.

"Neither of us had any experience of running a company or managing finance or managing anything for that matter!"

Kuch naya karenge, achha karenge – there was a sense of adventure.

Luckily, this mindset was also shared by the investor. The first time Mr Poddar sat down with the young entrepreneurs, he asked one simple question.

"*Apna* project *tees gaadi ka hai,* start *mein teen gaadi to nikal jayegi na*? (Our project capacity is 30 trucks, can you start with at least 3 trucks a day?)"

Puneet nodded 'yes'.

"*Theek hai – toh baaki saal bhar baad dekhenge.* (We will review the situation after one year)."

Rome wasn't built in a day and neither is an enterprise.

The initial plan was to set up the plant and begin manufacturing by the first quarter of 2009. But that did not happen. While civil construction started on schedule, it had to be stopped. The factory site was in Palsana taluka

"Initial years *main toh sab kuch ekdum* innovation *sa lagta tha*, even doing things which are very common in the industry."

"I think the best asset I could get from IIT Kharagpur was confidence that I can do anything."

of Surat district. The villagers nearby launched a protest that smoke from the factory would affect their crops.

"We made a presentation to the Ghaluda village panchayat, explaining the various pollution-control measures. But they were adamant."

Hence, a decision was taken to shift the factory site. As a result, the entire project got delayed by 6 months.

During this period, the young entrepreneurs were also busy arranging the ₹10 crore of debt required for the project. The bank which placed its faith in these freshers was the State Bank of India (SBI).

"I remember how it felt to get that first loan – *ki yaar* bank *ne* ₹10 crore pass *kar diya* based on our own credentials. That was something huge!"

As newcomers in the field, every day was a day of learning, of discovery. While importing machinery, it is common to take debt from the bank at 12-13% interest. However, Sourabh stumbled upon a concept called 'buyer's line of credit'. Using this, funds are available for as little as LIBOR* + 0.5%.

"When we realised *ki* we can borrow at 2% interest cost, we felt like *ki yaar ye toh koi jaadu nikla hai* (we felt it was like magic)."

However, such borrowings must be hedged to offset the risk of losses. This is usually done by taking a forward contract** at a cost of 7-8%. Further research revealed that a 'call' spread could reduce this cost, although it carried a little more risk.

* LIBOR is a benchmark rate that some of the world's leading banks charge each other for short-term loans.

** A forward contract is an agreement to buy or sell an asset on a specified date for a specified price.

"Like this, we were able to get financed at a cost of 4-5%!"

The next big challenge was how to actually import the machinery. The latest technology was available in China but identifying a good supplier is not easy. Especially when the entire deal is negotiated through an interpreter.

There are good vendors and there are bad vendors - you have to differentiate between the two. *Phir thoda* trust *karna hi padta hai*. (You have to trust someone).

"Luckily for us, even though it was our first experience dealing with the Chinese, it proved to be good."

In April 2009, civil construction began at the factory site in Arak village, Navsari district. The following month, machinery arrived and, in October 2009, Magicrete was ready to start production. As the first AAC blocks rolled out of the factory, the boys were faced with a big question: *kharidega kaun?*

"We thought that people who are already buying AAC blocks will take our product also, but that market was very small."

The big opportunity was converting the users of bricks into users of blocks. And it wasn't just about price. Brick is a 1000-year-old technology, the builder is comfortable with it. Change never comes easy.

"People used to ask questions like, plastering *sahi se hoga ki nahi,* nailing *hoga ki nahi, gir to nahin jayegi* building! (How will we put the plaster, how will we put the nails and what if the building collapses!)"

The proof the pudding lies in eating it. Rajesh Poddar became the first customer for his own product - he used AAC blocks in one of his upcoming real estate projects.

"The challenge now before us is how to build fences around our business."

"Blocks are just ₹30 per sq feet, we want to capture the entire ₹70 spent on building a wall."

He then introduced his young partners to Raghuveer Developers, a construction giant in Surat.

Sourabh arrived for the meeting, full of confidence. After all, he was an IIT graduate selling a revolutionary product. The key selling point of AAC blocks - in his opinion - was the fact that they are 'green'* and 'energy efficient' products.

5 minutes into the meeting, his idealism was shattered.

"Sitting in front of that customer, I realised *ki* builder *ko usse koi matlab nahin hai ki* whether your product is green, whether your product is energy efficient, builder *ko isse matlab hai ki* what value is he deriving out of the product."

The client showed the young engineer the calculation for a 100 square foot wall - 450 bricks, 6% mortar. So on and so forth, down to the last *naya paisa*. Sourabh did not have a counter-calculation ready.

"That was the day of realisation *ki* I need to do my homework properly."

He returned to the office, sat down and drafted a cost-comparison statement - 4-inch brick wall versus 4-inch block wall, 9-inch brick wall versus 9-inch block wall - what would be the actual cost per square foot? The company then got a structural engineer to write a case study on a building made purely with AAC blocks. The engineer estimated that such a structure would use 15% steel.

"The steel saving alone reduces the cost of construction by ₹25 per sq feet. So that was a huge value proposition."

* AAC blocks can be produced with 20% of the energy required to make a conventional brick.

The numbers were certainly convincing enough for Raghuveer Developers - they immediately started using blocks in all their projects. Other local developers followed suit. From Surat, the company decided to venture into the mega-market of Mumbai. Which was, in fact, relatively easy, because builders were already using Siporex AAC blocks.

The challenge in Mumbai was availability - Siporex enjoyed a monopoly and was unable to meet demand. Distributors were ready to stock Magicrete's AAC blocks, as their price was far more attractive.

"We also met architects to convince them we will be able to supply the right quantities at the right time."

In fact, Siporex is a part of the B G Shirke construction group and the plant's primary purpose was to supply material for their own projects. Whereas, for Magicrete, selling AAC blocks was the whole and soul of their business. Thus, in the very first year of operations, the company managed ₹8 crore in sales. Which was excellent, but the plant was still operating at only 30% of its capacity. The company needed to expand to new markets like Ahmedabad and Vadodara. But one general cannot lead on multiple fronts.

"Managing production as well as travelling all over for sales became a challenge. I realised that we needed to build a team - a great team as capable or more capable than me!"

Every entrepreneur is looking for the 'right people'. The question is - where do you find them?

Sourabh turned to his batchmates from IIT Kharagpur. They had taken jobs from the campus but he offered them something 'more'. The chance to be part of a great adventure.

The first to join was P V S Srikant, a year junior to Sourabh but from the same hostel. His mission - as head of marketing in Mumbai - was to go forth and conquer the western region. Next came Gaurav Sengar, a batchmate who was running his own venture but not getting much traction.

"I visit the factory once in 3 months now, because there is a system, there is a team in charge."

Sourabh proposed to him, "*Tu yahan aa ja, saath main mil ke karte hain,* grow *karte hain* - we are well funded. (Let's join hands and work together, grow together)."

Around the same time, Sourabh got married to Shweta and she, too, came on board. Putting her MBA to good use by starting new product lines within the company.

"I feel Shweta has been my lucky charm!" says Sourabh.

By March 2011, the company turnover had grown four-fold to ₹31 crore. Magicrete's first factory had a capacity of 150,000 cubic meters - that was doubled - then, a second factory was put up right next door. These units catered to the demand in the entire western region (in a 250 km radius). The time had come to expand further.

"We decided to set up a third factory near Delhi, to cater to the NCR market."

With the help of Google Maps, the team identified Jhajjar (Haryana) as an ideal location. Since it is situated close to a power plant, there is a regular supply of fly ash, an important raw material for AAC blocks. Jhajjar is also at a reasonable distance from several important markets such as Jaipur, Agra and Chandigarh.

"At this point, Sidharth joined the company and we decided to approach investors."

After graduating from IIM Lucknow, Sidharth had worked with McKinsey and then with Lighthouse - a private equity firm. Thus, he had a good understanding of how the PE industry works. This helped the young company immensely.

The first pitch was to Lighthouse - they showed interest and quickly offered a term sheet. However, through Sidharth's contacts with Avendus i-bank, the deal was taken to several other private equity players. In March 2013, Motilal

Oswal Private Equity invested ₹35 crore in Magicrete to fund further expansion.

"When we were seeking investors, their first concern always used to be – how good is the team. So that's where having a professional degree and IIT brand name certainly helps."

However, it was the rapid growth of the company in a short span of 5 years that really made it 'hot' property. The year-ending turnover in March 2013 was an impressive ₹100 crore – and the team is quite matter-of-fact about it.

"Actually, the path we are following was conceptualised in 2007-08. When we made our business plan, we had it in mind that, someday, we will have 8-10 factories."

In any line of business, there is a steep learning curve. Like a pilgrim, you must climb that mountain with faith and fortitude – there is no 'helicopter' service.

"*Paanch saal toh* business *ko seekhne main lag jata hai.* (It takes 5 years to master any business). Then, you really start growing."

Yet another IITian joined the rapidly growing company in November 2012. A mechanical engineer, one year senior to Sourabh at Kharagpur, Siddharth Sharma now leads Magicrete's strategic operations. From the very top to the very bottom, this is a merit-based organisation.

"For any position in the company, we advertise in the newspaper, candidates appear for tests, followed by an interview."

Selections at Magicrete are not based on 'who knows whom' but 'who knows what'. Plus, who is eager and willing to learn. A majority of the employees are local BCom graduates, with two full-time CAs on the rolls.

On the finance front, the biggest learning has been managing the cash flow.

"*Ek* running company *mein* there is always that fight between payments and collections," admits Puneet.

In the initial period, money, which was due in 7 days, would often arrive after 2-3 months. This created a lot of tension. Slowly, the situation came under control, through stricter monitoring and systems.

"We now have a strong ERP in place. If a payment is overdue, the next shipment is automatically put on hold."

Tricks of the trade are not taught in a classroom, but through hard-learnt, hard-earned experience.

In March 2014, Magicrete crossed ₹130 crore in revenue and counts more than 1500 developers as clients. But, competition has heated up. There are more than 50 AAC plants now operating in the country. Margins have, therefore, fallen drastically - from 40% to 20%.

So how does one build 'fences' around the business?

"We are entering new regions like Orissa and Karnataka where there are still very few plants."

However, the real focus is on moving beyond. The company has started two more verticals - dry mortar and prefabricated construction (factory-built homes). The young entrepreneurs believe that, in time, there will be a labour shortage. Making on-site construction a costly affair.

"We will see a day when factory *se bane banaye* solutions site *par jayenge* - it will be prefab everywhere!"

One aspect of the business - which the team takes pride in - is its impact on the environment. AAC blocks are manufactured from fly ash, a waste product generated by steel and power plants.

"We reuse millions of tons of fly ash and we make money from it... That's wealth from waste!"

The young entrepreneurs intend to take the company public in 2-3 years' time. There is ambition but there is also awareness about *other* important aspects of life - family, friends, fatherhood. Both the Bansals and Puneet are proud papas to young baby girls. Feeding bottles and changing nappies are a part of life - especially for Sourabh, with twin newborn babies at home!

"My dad always said, there are 6 spokes of life - finance,

family, society, physical, emotional and spiritual health. You have to consciously maintain a balance."

People will say, *yeh nahin ho sakta, woh nahin ho sakta*. But anything is possible.

If your mind can conceive it, your heart can believe it, you *can* achieve it... Try *kar ke toh dekho*!

ADVICE TO YOUNG ENTREPRENEURS

Sourabh

First advice would be, think big. While I was in college, I wrote down '₹5000 crore' next to my bed and people used to say, *kya likh raha hai, pagal hai kya, koi soch sakta hai kya.* I thought *ki yaar* this is a number that could be achieved, my father's business was hardly a crore of rupees then, but still I dared to think *ki haan pahunch sakte hain.*

So 'dream big' and, of course, put in all efforts, keep on innovating and striving toward your goal. Take the plunge early. The age of 20-30 years are the most dynamic years of life – make the best use of them!

Puneet

Think big and work hard. There is no replacement for hard work, but start *karne se pehle uska ek* roadmap *hona chahiye*. At least, initial 2-3 *saal ki apko bahut* clarity *honi chahiye, ki* how will you move forward (you need to have a roadmap for the first 2-3 years).

Jo start *kiya*, you have to stick to that for first 2-3 years, 5 years, and then go forward and be gutsy!!

Sidharth

After the first 3-4 years of starting up, it is most important to professionalise the business. Raising outside capital from private equity funds/institutional investors and getting outside professionals in key positions, are critical in scaling the business to the next level.

Entrepreneurs should always focus on 'making the system work'. The indicator of depth in management is that the founding team should be able to take a 15 to 30 days' break and the business should grow even in their absence.

And most importantly: Always run a tight and lean ship. Do not burden the business with unnecessary costs, overheads like fancy offices, high travel costs and wasteful expenditure.

GIFT OF THE GAB

Prakash Mundhra (SCMHRD, Pune)
SACRED MOMENTS

He entered a business-plan competition, just for fun. He exited campus with a ready-to-launch business. 8 years on, Prakash Mundhra is the CEO of a ₹4.5 crore company and has no regrets.

SCMHRD is a go-to place for anyone who wants to be an HR professional. Like any other MBA institute, a 'good job' is a badge of honour.

Prakash Mundhra entered the program with this very goal, yet, at the end of two years, he turned his back on a job. Because he had an 'option'.

It all started with a business-plan contest, one of many such contests on campus. For Prakash, it became something 'more'. A passion, an obsession, a ticket to national television.

"I participated in Zee TV's 'Business Baazigar' show and made it to the final 10."

In his second year of college, Prakash won several B-plan contests and pocketed close to ₹1.5 lakh in prize money. By the end of his MBA, he had two birds in hand – a job *and* a business idea. He chose the business.

Prakash used his two years in B-school to research and refine his idea, build a prototype. By the time he graduated, he was confident – this will work!

8 years later, Sacred Moments has morphed into a corporate gifting company. And Prakash is a savvy businessman. But he looks back fondly on those early days.

"I am glad I worked on my idea when I was still a student – it gave me a head start."

If you have an idea in your head, just start. It may go here, or there, or nowhere. But it just might give you 'futures' and 'options'.

GIFT OF THE GAB

Prakash Mundhra (SCMHRD, Pune)
SACRED MOMENTS

Prakash Mundhra was born in Ranchi and spent his early years in Kolkata.

"I belong to the Marwari-Maheshwari community who are primarily into business. We were in the cotton textile line."

Prakash grew up in a joint family with his grandfather, uncles and cousins staying together in Kolkata's Bara Bazaar area. A student of the well-known Shri Daulatram Nopany Vidyalaya, he excelled in academics from Class 4 onward.

"Like all boys, I loved cricket, He-Man, 'Ramayana' and 'Quiz Time'. But overall, I was a very disciplined and well-behaved child."

In 1994, the family business expanded and Prakash shifted to Thane with his parents and siblings. He took up the science stream after Class 10 with the goal of becoming an engineer. But this dream came crashing down when, after a freak accident, he could not appear for the board exam.

"Since I used to participate in lots of quiz contests, I read the biographies of successful business tycoons. It also gave me quite a few life lessons."

"I was shattered to lose a crucial year but I also learnt an important lesson. Troubles come without warning and you have to bounce back!"

At this point, Prakash decided to drop science and switch to commerce. After scoring 80% in the HSC exam, he took admission in the newly-launched Bachelor of Management Studies (BMS) course at Sydenham College, Churchgate, Mumbai.

"I was part of many extracurricular activities in college such as the Sydenham Book Circle and various quiz competitions."

During these years, the family business went through a rough patch. Hence, it made more sense to go for an MBA and join the corporate world. From TYBMS, Prakash was focused on CAT and related entrance exams. But, despite his best efforts, he failed to get admission to any top-tier B-school.

"Either I would just miss the cut-off or get eliminated at the interview stage. The two years after graduation were a real struggle."

During this time, Prakash joined his family business and even did a short course at the Micro, Small & Medium Enterprises Development Institute (MSME) but somehow could not get over his MBA obsession. He decided to give it one last shot and this time, made it to SCMHRD (Symbiosis Centre for Management and Human Resource Development).

"The MBA initial experience was great as it was the first time that I was living away from home."

Prakash was an above-average student but not one of the toppers. However, he was able to make a mark as a 'knowledge powerhouse', thanks to his interest in biographies and business magazines.

During the first semester of the first year, the ITC '*Mera Gaon Mera Desh*' B-plan contest became the talk of the campus. Students from top B-schools were invited to come up with a new rural business idea for ITC around its existing products. At stake was not just prize money, but a direct placement with the company.

While most students chose to make a plan related to e-Choupal*, Prakash was thinking differently. Looking at the ITC, product portfolio, he saw 'Mangaldeep Agarbatti' and made up his mind to focus on it for one simple reason.

"Agarbatti was the only product which I could easily understand."

It did not take Prakash long to come up with a simple business plan proposing branded puja items such as *roli*, *haldi* and even religious tourism. The logic was, what Amul has done for milk, Mangaldeep can do for religious products.

"We made a grand plan which looked great in Excel but it was rejected in the first round itself."

The result was disappointing but the experience of making the B-plan and searching for opportunities gave Prakash a thrill. Something he was keen to experience again.

"The year we joined MBA, there was news of Vardan Kabra from IIMA refusing placement to start a school. So the trend of entrepreneurship had begun."

* E-choupal is an ITC initiative which allows farmers to directly sell their produce to buyers through the internet.

"MBA case studies are larger than life, so students start thinking 'strategy' from Day 1. But, in business, execution also matters a lot."

The habit of visiting the college library came in handy when Prakash came across a news item about 'Business Baazigar': a show on Zee TV seeking innovative business ideas from common people.

"I thought of submitting the puja products' B-plan after tweaking it - after all, we get expert in tweaking our MBA projects!"

First, Prakash changed the brand name to 'Shubh Labh' and since the idea had to be innovative, he came up with the idea of a 'puja kit' for different occasions, for instance, one for Diwali, another for weddings, and so on. This, he felt, would be a product of great interest to the younger generation.

"I could see that my generation is inclined towards puja, but they want it to be a hassle-free experience."

Of the two lakh business plans submitted to 'Business Baazigar', 500 were selected for the second round. The Shubh Labh 'puja kit' was one of them. Following interviews and further eliminations, Prakash found himself in the top 50 and then, among the top 20, contestants.

"The rest of my class was to attend a 10-day Vipassana course - luckily our director, Subbu Sir, allowed me to skip it and focus on the show instead."

The top 20 contestants were each given ₹50,000 to do a pilot project and make a 'working model' or sample. This gave Prakash the freedom to hire a designer as well as travel to meet raw-material suppliers, pundits and retailers. Prakash was, thus, able to build a prototype puja kit and submit it to 'Business Baazigar'.

"This pilot project gave me knowledge of costing, quality of raw materials, market size, competition and procurement policies of modern retail."

In February 2005, shooting for the show commenced in Mumbai*. Initially, it was about fun and light activities but, slowly, participants were given challenges to test their business acumen. After each round, a few were eliminated. Prakash made it to the top 10 before exiting the show as a 'Mini Baazigar'.

"I was one of the 3 contestants who got this special title because the judges felt *ki idea mein dum hai*."

The interaction with other participants made Prakash more confident of his business plan. It was realistic and it was possible without venture funding.

Prakash went back to campus and refined his idea – from branded puja items to branded puja kits. The NRI and gifting market seemed to be lucrative – there were so many possibilities! However, come December and the campus was gripped by placement fever.

"I could not make a decision at the time, so I sat for the placement and got into two companies – ICICI Prudential and Essar."

But while his classmates chilled out in the final semester, Prakash spent most of his time working on puja kits. And participating in business-plan contests. He took part in 6 such contests and won 5 of them, including IIM Lucknow, TAPMI and IIT Kharagpur.

"I felt that I have the option to go big if I get funding but in case I don't get any monetary support, I could still start on my own."

* 'Business Baazigar' was telecast on Zee TV between March 2006 and August 2006.

"When one of my exams at SCMHRD was clashing with a business-plan contest, I ditched the exam."

"I felt, I am definitely on the right track!"

Feedback from judges in these B-plan contests also helped him immensely.

Now came the moment of truth - will it be the job or the business? Prakash was to join ICICI Pru on 11 May 2006. On 7 May, he sent them an email declining the offer. Thus 'Sacred Moments' was born.

Prakash needed ₹6 lakh to start the business. The prize money from various B-plan contests he'd won was close to ₹2 lakh, the rest he borrowed from his father, who supported him wholeheartedly.

"I chose the name 'Blessingz' for the puja kits and started making branded samples."

Prakash consulted 3-4 pundits and decided to come out with a Diwali puja kit. Each kit includes 32 items used on Diwali, including a *murti*, *haldi*, *roli*, *mishri* and even *Gangajal*. A *vidhi* booklet also tells you how to perform the puja.

The first samples were displayed at the Giftex exhibition in Mumbai between 3 and 7 August 2006.

"I got a really good response as well as the 'best new product' award. However, I got mainly enquiries and not actual bookings."

At this point, Prakash took a bold decision. He decided to go ahead and manufacture 12,000 kits. The kits were prepared on a job work basis; the assembly of items was also outsourced. Prakash used his dad's old office in Masjid Bunder as a base.

The biggest challenge at this time was coordinating with 40 suppliers all across India for various items in the puja kit. The sector is unorganised and delivery time is always an issue.

"Even if one item is delayed, the assembly line comes to a halt!"

One of the items in the kit was a 20-gram sachet of ghee. Everyone told Prakash it wasn't available in Mumbai - why not simply drop it? But that didn't seem right. Prakash scoured the internet and finally found someone in Tirupur who packs ghee sachets for hotel parcel service.

Then there were small details like, how do you keep the photo of the God upright? Prakash decided to provide a small photo stand. However, all ideas could not be implemented due to cost issues.

"One client wanted a silver coin but that was uneconomical so we gave a silver *durva* (grass) instead."

Meanwhile, orders started trickling in. Corporate clients included *The Times of India* group, Ultratech Cement, Linc Pens and Piramal Healthcare. In the run up to Diwali, Blessingz kits were also stocked at the Asiatic and Akbarallys department stores in Mumbai.

"I sold 10,000 kits by Diwali. Strangely enough, I got around 500 orders even after Diwali!"

A Punjabi family, for example, gave it to all their *baraatis* as a gift. Others bought the kit to present after *Bhaagwat katha*. IMT Nagpur gave it to delegates at a conference on their campus.

Working capital was tight but a few suppliers gave credit, while corporates gave an advance. Despite that, Prakash had

"Everybody thought the puja kit idea was just to win B-plan contests and win some prize money. But it had entered deep in my veins."

"MBA gave me optimism as well as techniques to work around problems."

to borrow ₹3 lakh from 4 friends just before Diwali – he repaid them soon after.

The gamble of manufacturing 12,000 kits brought handsome dividends.

"I sold 4000 kits in the last week before Diwali. If I did not have the kits ready, I would have missed that business."

The gross revenues were ₹35 lakh (at ₹350 each) with ₹5 lakh in profit. This was equal to the money he would have earned in a job.

"In fact, I could have earned more but because I was new to business I made a lot of small and big mistakes."

After Diwali, Prakash took a 3-month break – to help with his sister's marriage as well as his own. In the new year, he focused attention back into the business but now came a fresh challenge – Diwali was months away. In the meanwhile, what should he sell?

Prakash toyed with several ideas – lower-priced kits (₹200) for the retail mass market, *griha pravesh puja* kits, vehicle puja kits, and so on. Meanwhile, he went back to his clients and asked, "What kind of items do you need?"

"I realised that many pharma companies were having difficulty in getting customised textile products like towels and handkerchiefs."

This was the business his father and brother were already engaged in – all they had to do was add logo weaving.

Prakash also began exploring the export market for the puja kits business. With more orders coming in, he decided to shift partial production to Ahmedabad – where the manufacturing cost was lower.

Opportunity doesn't always knock, it talks. Chatting with

merchants and exporters, Prakash discovered that they were facing a problem supplying clay diyas. There was a high percentage of breakage during transportation.

"I decided to supply clay diyas with 'safety guarantee' due to better packing."

To do this, Prakash set up a small unit at Thane to start painting and decorating clay diyas and manufacturing religious handicrafts such as *toran*, *rangoli* and *thali*. He reached out to importers in the US, UK, South Africa, Zimbabwe and Australia, inviting them to stop by at his unit during their India visit. In this manner, he was able to procure a good number of bulk orders.

In 2009, a family friend joined a company which is the sole authorised importer and distributor of 9 luxury perfume brands like Bvlgari, Hermès and Guess, in India. This rang a bell in his mind. People like to buy brands at a discount but they have a doubt – is the product genuine?

"I was able to offer my corporate clients an institutional discount along with a guarantee of authenticity."

Thus, the venture morphed into a 'gift items' business with puja kit as one of the items. But while the general trend is to be a dealer of 100 products and cater to 100 clients, Prakash chose the difficult path of dealing with 1000 clients with a limited 8 to 10 products.

Yet, by March 2014, Sacred Moments had clocked a turnover of ₹4.5 crore (with 45% coming from puja kits and other religious products). At present, there are 7 permanent employees and a flexible staff of 25 people who work on daily wages during the 'season', that is, from July to October when demand for puja items peaks.

"Because I was new to business, I made a lot of small and big mistakes."

"I have absolutely no regrets, I enjoy my work, learn something new each day!"

It's the other items which keep business chugging all year round! Thus, Prakash is always on the lookout for 'something new' to add to his portfolio.

"I concentrate only in the B2B market and search for a gap where I can provide better packaging or better service."

As a thumb rule, Prakash prefers products which are sample-able and courier-able, so that he can access buyers all over the world. He also does an MBA-style SWOT* analysis - What is the demand curve for a product over the past 5 years? How much competition can be expected from China?

Funding the expansion is a sleeping partner who invests but does not participate in the day-to-day management. But the next line of business - plastic packaging products - Prakash is ready to finance with accruals.

"So far I have taken neither term loans nor working capital from any bank."

Life is as hectic as it would be in a corporate job, with a 10-hour working day, Monday to Saturday, and 3 hours on Sunday. But it's more satisfying, more challenging.

"I have absolutely no regrets, I enjoy my work, learn something new each day!"

Despite the pressures of business, Prakash takes time out to 'give back' to society. He is vice-president of the Thane Maheshwari Yuva Samiti, a community youth organisation, and often gives guest lectures on entrepreneurship at B-schools.

And yes, at the end of the day, this young entrepreneur is able to spend quality time with his loved ones.

---

* SWOT = Strength, Weakness, Opportunity, Threat analysis.

"I continue to live in a joint family and they are my biggest support system."

Prakash continues to read management books and enjoys listening to TED talks. Because, inspiration and ideas are everywhere.

You don't have to hide behind a tree like Eklavya to observe Guru Dronacharya. Choose your own gurus, follow their words, their deeds, their feats.

It's the best 'gift' you will ever give yourself!

ADVICE TO YOUNG ENTREPRENEURS

Do not hesitate to get into business directly after B-school or college, especially if your work area is such that corporate experience would not matter much.

We have heard many stories of entrepreneurship from IIM, but non-IIM students need to have a strong belief that it is your learning during the MBA course which matters and not the IIM tag when it comes to being an entrepreneur.

You may at times be required to fool outsiders for keeping your business alive but never try to fool yourself in your own business. It is easier nowadays to hog the limelight even for a concept which is not working, but entrepreneurship is not about being featured in news channels or magazines.

Accept that you will not be good at everything. Admit it, take help.

Never scrounge on something which is crucial to the success of your business. For example, I hired a professional designer although DTP operators were much cheaper because the design of the box was crucial for my puja kit.

Have a positive attitude and perseverance during tough times. Only perseverance is not enough as negative thinking creates negative results.

Believe in the power of marketing - use the internet, social media marketing and telecommunication to your advantage.

REPEATERS

The dudes who tried – and failed – but had the will to try again. Because nothing that is worth anything comes easily. And giving up is *not* an option.

Prabhkiran Singh

Siddharth Munot

TWO IDIOTS

Prabhkiran Singh & Siddharth Munot
(IIT Bombay)
BEWAKOOF BRANDS

As a third-year IIT student, Prabhkiran Singh started selling flavoured lassi. The venture failed, but taught him many important lessons about life. The 'lassiwallah' now runs a ₹5 crore youth-focused online business.

In the year 1999, Kanwal Rekhi set up an incubator at IIT Bombay - one of the first initiatives to encourage entrepreneurship on campus. Students and faculty came forward with ideas related to technology - algorithms, robotics, semi-conductors, internet solutions, to name a few.

Bhai, IIT *hai - kuch dimaag wala kaam to hona chahiye*!

Along came Prabhkiran Singh - a lad from Ludhiana who started a lassi business. Right outside the IIT gate. 'Khadke Glassi' made waves on campus and even became a national news item.

The common refrain was, "*Bhai, yehi karna tha toh* IIT *kyon* join *kiya*. This is waste of a seat!"

As luck would have it, the lassi business tanked. But Prabhkiran teamed up with his batchmate, Siddharth, and got into the T-shirt business. Which then morphed into Bewakoof.com - an irreverent brand for the youth.

Today, the young entrepreneurs sell funky clothing and accessories online - with orders crossing ₹1 crore a month. The Bewakoof brand has largely been built through its Facebook page with over 1.4 million followers (none of them paid).

You don't need to be an IIT grad to start such a business - you need to be confident, you need to be bold. You need to be different and break the mould.

'Success' is like JEE, except there's no coaching. Just choose the door you want and keep knocking!

TWO IDIOTS

Prabhkiran Singh & Siddharth Munot
(IIT Bombay)
BEWAKOOF BRANDS

Prabhkiran Singh was born and brought up in Ludhiana.

"My dad was in business and my mom is a housewife. I studied in Sacred Heart Convent School."

After Class 10, Prabhkiran went to Kota for IIT coaching. Actually, at that time, he had no idea *ki* IIT *hai kya*. He just went because his friends were going.

"It was only later that I came to know the importance of IIT, so I became serious and studied hard for it."

Prabhkiran opted for civil engineering - not the most preferred branch. But he was excited because it had always been his dream to go to Mumbai.

The first and second year at IIT Bombay were fairly routine. In the third year came the time for internship. At IIT, this is an important time, when students start thinking, *aage kya karna hai?* (what should I do in life?). While most of his batchmates were choosing between finance, consulting and technical jobs, Prabhkiran was on a completely different trip.

He did apply to the first company which came on campus - Deutsche Bank - but did not get shortlisted. Although disappointed, he was also relieved. The pre-placement talk made the job sound so constrained and boring - was he really cut out for it?

"*Bas*, after that, I stopped applying to jobs. I decided to start something of my own."

But where does one start? One day at Crossword Bookshop, Prabhkiran came across a book called *Stay Hungry Stay Foolish.* It featured the success stories of entrepreneurs from IIM Ahmedabad. He bought it, read it and re-read it.

"*Stay Hungry* was my first non-fiction book and it inspired me a lot. After that, I read *Polyester Prince* (Dhirubhai Ambani's story), *It Happened in India* (Kishore Biyani) and many others."

The first thing you need to start a business is a business idea. Prabhkiran spent 3-4 months looking for that 'killer idea', but almost anything he thought of had already been done. Or didn't excite him.

Around this time, Prabhkiran happened to make 2-3 train journeys. During these trips, he happened to sample 'flavoured lassi' – strawberry lassi in Pune and rose lassi in Agra. Now, this was interesting! Lassi flows in the veins of every Punjabi *puttar* but it is either sweet or salty. The idea of lassi with flavours caught the young man's fancy.

"I was fascinated by the Starbucks story and in India we have Jumbo King. I thought we can do something similar, but with lassi."

It was October 2009. Prabhkiran roped in his best friend Himanshu Dhiman to work on the idea. Thanks to some events organised by the IIT Bombay E-Cell, the boys knew about something called a 'business plan'.

At that time, everyone was like, if you have a good idea, you will get funding. If you have a good business plan, you can go out and start!"

But how does one actually make this plan? You can enter any number on that Excel sheet but how do you know it's 'right'? There is no logic, no formula which tells you *pehle mahine kitna bikega, doosre mahine kitna bikega*. The boys were mighty confused.

"Then we thought, during the summer break, we will raise

₹2 lakh from friends and family and with that, we will start an outlet."

They started planning *kya karenge, kaise karenge* – slowly, steadily. But everything changed on 18 February 2010. Prabhkiran met a gentleman called Devashish Chakravorty who gave him a piece of practical advice.

"If you have a product, start selling it!"

Wow – could it be as simple as that? Then and there, Prabhkiran decided to 'just do it' and set a deadline of 3 days. Himanshu contributed his monthly pocket money (₹5000) and Prabhkiran did the same (₹3000). With this grand sum, they bought a cheap mixer, a blender and some utensils. But where would they sell from?

The boys roamed up and down the streets of Powai, looking for premises. But shop rentals ranged from ₹20,000 to ₹40,000 per month, with a ₹2 lakh deposit to boot. Way beyond their reach.

"Then we tried the *subzi mandi* outside the IIT gate but even that place is reserved for hawkers who pay BMC, so it did not work out."

Finally, they stumbled upon a newly opened cake shop whose business was yet to pick up. There was a small space outside the shop which was unutilised. The boys approached the owner with an offer – let us use this space, we will pay you ₹6000 as 'rent'.

"We gave ₹2000 advance and said, 'Once we start earning, we will pay the rest.' And he agreed to that!"

There were still a couple of problems, like what would be the menu? For the next 4-5 days frantic experiments were

"My parents wanted me to go to IIT Delhi because it is closer to my hometown, but I wanted to come to Mumbai."

"There is a myth that you need a fancy business plan and a big investor to start a business. You have to somehow start!"

conducted in the hostel room using curd stolen from the student mess. Friends tasted and reviewed various flavours before the final 4 were selected - chocolate, strawberry, rose and grape (ice cream optional).

The last issue was procuring a counter. A stainless steel table would cost ₹25-30,000, which they could not afford. Finally, they improvised with an old computer table and covered it with sunpac board.

"To make it more attractive, we printed graphics of 'Punjab' and 'lassi' on the sunpac and that did the job!"

Thus, on 23 February 2010, 'Khadke Glassi' went into business. With the help of a Facebook page and word of mouth publicity, there was a long line of customers. *Dekhte hain sardar kar kya raha hai.*

On the very first day, 44 glasses of lassi were sold for ₹25 each.

But there were no elation, no celebration. By the end of the evening, Himanshu had decided to quit, sending Prabhkiran into shock. Somehow, he pulled himself together and opened shop the next day. And the next, and the next.

"We had our labs till 5 pm, so every day I used to open only between 5 pm to 10 pm."

Initially, Prabhkiran found it very difficult. He was an introvert by nature, talking to people did not come naturally. Over and above, there was the matter of pride. How would batchmates react, seeing one of their own doing this 'manual work'?

"I was scared and hesitant but people responded very well."

While a few did snigger, most thought it was cool. Some

even came up and hugged him, saying, "*Hum log to bolte rehte hain, tumne kar ke dikhaya*!"

All this boosted Prabhkiran's morale. But, in about 10 days time, friends got busy and stopped coming. The number of customers per day dropped, and so did the young entrepreneur's enthusiasm.

"We had our quizzes and exams coming up but I had to be at the counter every single day. Even Saturdays and Sundays."

The answer was to hire someone but it wasn't easy. Labour coming from outside the city needs a place to stay – this he could not provide. Workers from Mumbai need at least a month to quit their current jobs.

"I thought I would be serving lassi for a week but I actually did it for 42 days. That required tremendous discipline."

On 14 March 2010, *The Times of India,* Mumbai edition, carried a story titled 'IITian Scores with Lassi Bar'. Overnight Khadke Glassi became 'famous'. Customers from in and around the locality thronged the outlet. Business was brisk with 150 glasses getting sold per day.

"I had to request a friend to come and help out!"

The news reached Ludhiana in a dramatic fashion. Prabhkiran's brother was doing MBA in Ludhiana, the professor came to the class, dropped the newspaper on the table and said, "Look at this fellow, he is from Punjab and doing lassi business in Mumbai. *Tum sab kisi kaam ke nahin*! (You are all useless fellows!)."

Prabhkiran's parents were shocked. *Kya issi kaam ke liye puttar ko humne* IIT *bheja? Aur hamein khabar akhbaar se*

"After selling lassi, I have become *besharam*. There is no situation in life that can make me uncomfortable."

"If you have money, you can get someone to build your website. Otherwise, you have to build it yourself! "

miley? (Is this why we sent you to IIT? And that too, we come to know about it from the newspaper?)

"Actually, my dad was in business but when I was in school, he suffered a big loss and shut it down. That's why he wanted me to join IIT and take a job."

But Singh saab realised there was a bright side to the story. Mumbai *jaa kar bachcha bhatak bhi sakta tha.* (Any young man can go astray in a city like Mumbai). *Chalo*, at least the boy is doing something useful, *kuch to seekhega* (he will learn something).

"I told him not to worry – this is just for fun – I will ultimately take up a job."

And thus the lassi kept churning at stone's throw from IIT Gate No. 1. One of the regular customers at Khadke Glassi was Siddharth Munot – he used to stop by for chocolate lassi.

"Actually, we were both third year, both civil, but different hostels. We knew each other by face but we weren't really friends."

In fact, the two shared a lot in common. Like Prabhkiran, Siddharth was a maverick. From his very first year at IIT, he was more interested in business than in a job. So, he started trying his hand at different things.

"The first thing that came to mind is, let me make some money online. Then I figured that it is not possible without any hard work."

Siddharth started learning how to make a website. He realised there was money to be made from Google AdSense – if you could attract enough visitors. To do this, he set up a virtual game where prizes were awarded to visitors at random. The site was called internetpaise.com and it started getting traffic. And then it became difficult to manage.

"I was replying to 70-80 mails a day with queries like, 'how to participate', 'what are the prizes' - so on and so forth. I got frustrated and shut it."

At the same time, Siddharth started taking physics classes at Pace Academy, a nearby IIT coaching centre. He really enjoyed teaching and, on weekends, he would take classes 7-8 hours at a stretch. The money was also good - up to ₹20,000 per month - and, initially, Siddharth dabbled in the stock market. But soon, he found a more interesting place to 'invest'.

"I started buying domain names - it became my hobby and my timepass."

The trick was to find a unique and 'saleable' name to purchase. Every 3-4 days, Siddharth would locate such a name and was often able to buy a domain for as little as ₹100.

In fact, Siddharth was always so occupied with various plans and projects that he never ever went home for vacation. The summer of 2010 was no different.

Around the same time, Prabhkiran's lassi business further heated up. A senior from IIT Bombay liked the concept of Khadke Glassi and agreed to invest in the business. The plan was to open 10 outlets in ₹10 lakh but before doing that, the investor put the model to one final test.

"He gave me ₹50,000 to shift to the Galleria shopping centre which has higher footfalls - just to see the response."

The Galleria outlet opened in June 2010 and sales were excellent, despite higher prices. But once the monsoon set in, sales plummeted. From 50 glasses a day, business was down to 5 glasses a day. And the trend continued for the next 2 months.

In September 2010, Prabhkiran decided to take a break and shut down the outlet.

"The same people who once congratulated me, now said, '*Yeh to hona hi tha* (we knew he would fail)."

"The same people who once congratulated me now said, '*Yeh to hona hi tha* (we knew he would fail!)'."

But by this time, Prabhkiran had developed a thick skin and strong mind. He knew, *"Yeh nahi, kuch aur sahi*. There is something else for me out there."

Around this time, Prabhkiran teamed up with Siddharth for a social initiative called '*Purani* jeans *aur* T-shirt'. The mission was to reach out to every room in IIT and ask people to donate old clothes. The previous year, only 800-900 pieces were collected. This time, the number crossed 4000 – all of which were sent to the NGO, Goonj*.

"It was a good partnership, good team work... *itna toh* clear *ho gaya tha ki hum saath kaam kar sakte hain* (we felt we can do something together)."

At that time, Siddharth was also experimenting with a website he'd created called bewakoof.com. The idea was that people can come and share their *bewakoofi* and others can rate it, thus creating a '*bewakoofi* index'. To promote this website, Siddharth had made a T-shirt which he wore on campus.

Folks loved the T-shirt and wanted to know, "Where can we buy it?"

"Then, we thought this is a good business – *yehi karte hain*."

Thus, in October, Siddharth and Prabhkiran got into the T-shirt business. There was plenty of business on campus itself, with each hostel ordering 200-300 T-shirts every year. The boys roped in one of their juniors to help out. Soon after, they met two IITB alumni who were in the same line of business.

---

* The complete story of Goonj can be read in *I Have a Dream* by Rashmi Bansal.

"We decided to join hands and work as partners. So we registered a new private limited company."

The partnership lasted only 3 months, due to compatibility issues. It was back to square one. At this time, Siddharth toyed with the idea of 'online career consulting' as a business.

"Before I joined civil, I had no idea what it is, similar is the case with my students at the coaching centre. So I thought there will be good demand for this service."

Siddharth worked on the idea for a month – he made a website, flyers and even found a partner willing to give office space. But, within a month, that fellow backed out.

"We went back to our T-shirt business and after passing out in April 2011, we continued working on it."

The boys took up a two BHK flat in Powai which served as both home and 'office'. 50% of the orders were still coming from IIT Bombay – the rest through friends in other colleges. They also started pitching to companies. Not just T-shirts but any requirement, such as bags, badges, trophies. For each item the challenge was to locate the best (and lowest cost) supplier in Mumbai.

At this time, the company had a single employee and the partners had no clear division of 'who will do what'. The idea was to just keep showing results and then go for funding. But it wasn't easy.

"IIT *se jab nikle they tab tak jitna paisa kamaya tha voh* flat *ka* deposit *dene mein chala gaya*. (When we graduated, our entire profit till then went towards deposit of the flat)."

The deposit amount was ₹1 lakh.

"We used to go out and talk, whether in the day or in the night! We met any person possible who was interested in talking to us."

"*Shuru mein khane ka paisa bhi,* it was like, *idhar se udhaar, udhar se udhaar...* that was the situation. (In the initial period, we had to borrow money from here and there just to survive.)"

Things gradually improved and the business began generating ₹2 lakh monthly. The boys began the hunt for an angel investor. They spread the word with friends, alumni circles and made countless pitches.

"We used to go out and talk whether in the day or in the night! We met any person possible who was interested in talking to us."

Not all of them were receptive. Some even said, "IIT *ke baad yeh kya kar rahe ho* – you have wasted one seat!"

The lassi man shrugs – by now, used to it.

The other big challenge was how to convince investors in their 30s and 40s about the vision for a youth brand. Finally, they met an IIT senior who 'understood' and took a quick decision.

"At first glance, he was like, *haan tum kar sakte ho,* he had that confidence in us. Being from a Gujarati business class he could see *ki isme kuch dum hai*. This idea is working."

Thus, Bewakoof received its first small seed funding to 'do the same thing on a larger scale'. Part of this money was used to set up a printing unit. Outsourcing was convenient but printing the T-shirts yourself allowed you to experiment. And also do 'same day' production when required.

"When we got printing done outside, the suppliers used to make mistakes and even refused to give samples. So it was a big headache!"

Once the machine was in, they doubled the effort to get more orders. This meant cold calling at college festivals and corporates – lots of running around, printing and despatching. At the same time, the concept of Bewakoof was taking shape.

"Inspired by JAM magazine, we started a Bewakoof magazine with funny quotes and articles but later we decided to build the brand only through Facebook."

Come December and the famous Mood Indigo festival at IIT Bombay was around the corner. An ideal launchpad for Bewakoof merchandise. The boys booked a stall and, in 15 days flat, they had 300 T-shirts in 7 designs and assorted sizes. All bearing the black and yellow Bewakoof logo.

"We did not know what kind of response to expect so we made around 300 T-shirts thinking we might be able to sell half."

To their surprise, the entire stock sold out in two and a half days. The 'Ghanta Engineering' design was so popular that people would come to the stall and say, "Take my name and address - courier it to me."

And they paid in advance. This gave the young entrepreneurs an idea - why not have a website through which they could sell to college students all over India?

"Actually, we had thought of retailing our T-shirts through shops - that time e-commerce was not such a craze."

But seeing the response, they took a quick decision.

"We promised people that our website is launching in January - with many more designs!"

Bewakoof.com went online on the 10 February 2012 and in the very first month, around 50 T-shirts got sold. The products were despatched through couriers like DTDC or via Speedpost. A few consignments did get lost or misplaced but since the volume was low, the complaints were quickly resolved.

"We could give individual attention to the orders, we used to follow up - *mila hai ke nahi*. We learnt the importance of logistics in e-commerce business!"

"If you look around our office, you will hardly see anyone above the age of 25."

"When we started, we had sale of ₹1 lakh a month, now the monthly sale is often in excess of ₹1 crore."

As orders increased in number, Bewakoof.com switched to a more reliable courier - Blue Dart. To handle the increase in traffic, they also had to upgrade the backend of the website. While many freelance programmers were available on the IITB campus, the boys knew it would be a temporary arrangement. And that wouldn't do.

"It's tough to hire the right people but we decided, we need to have programmers with us full-time."

When you are selling something, you want people to know about it. But you don't want to be the guy shouting *'chai chai'* when the train rolls into the platform. You want to be a CCD - where people walk in and keep coming back.

"We have done quite well in building the brand Bewakoof through Facebook - apart from T-shirts, we give people fun and entertainment. So they keep looking forward - what next?"

The Bewakoof Facebook page is updated 15-20 times a day with topical humour, contributed by folks spread all over the country. Of course, this can and does create some difficulty. For example, political humour is very popular but politicians take it too seriously.

"After we got a couple of warnings from Facebook, we made a 'no politics' rule. Similarly, we avoid religion or any topic where people easily take offence!"

In less than a year, Bewakoof was selling 200-250 T-shirts a day, online. And unlike most e-commerce companies - it was profitable. The surprising part is that T-shirts were sourced from Mumbai itself. The advantage being an ability to work in 'real time'- *ki aaj* order *aaya hai, kal aa bhi jayega,* print *bhi ho jayega, chala bhi jayega* (once the order comes, we can print and despatch in a day).

"If you buy T-shirts from Ludhiana or Tirupur, transport itself will take 10 days!"

On April Fool's Day, Bewakoof.com offered a small discount and got 10 times the orders. Yet they were able to ship out the entire lot within 3 days. And keep the customers happy.

By March 2014, Bewakoof had added a range of new products - boxer shorts, pajamas, sweatshirts and a separate section for girls. As well as funky phone covers and laptop skins. The turnover for the year-ending March 2014 was over ₹5 crore and expected to double this year with further expansion.

"We are not a clothing company, we are a youth brand. So in 2-3 years, you might see Bewakoof cafes, Bewakoof TV - anything can happen but it's all about Bewakoof."

At present, the company has 150 employees - half in production and despatch and the rest in customer care, design and marketing. Bewakoof is also a hotspot for internships - dozens of IITians applied last year, of which 6 were selected.

In some important areas - like accounting - the company leans on professionals. However, even with a 'good CA', the entrepreneur must keep track *ki kya ho raha hai*.

"If you don't know your business inside out, anyone can take you for a ride!"

You gotta be street smart to outsmart those who label you 'too young', 'too dumb', 'too inexperienced'.

Bewakoof.com has grown pretty big, pretty fast. But the dream is much bigger. The company is looking to raise funds, looking to grow further.

"We definitely want to go public in the next 5 years..."

Jahanpanah tussi great ho - tohfa kabool karo! Har batch *aise* 2-4 idiots produce *karo!*

ADVICE TO YOUNG ENTREPRENEURS

Siddharth

One thing is that *mehnat toh karna padega*. Hard work *karte raho* persistently. Just keep doing, keep doing, keep doing. You should want to do it, keep motivating yourself!

Like *hum dono ke* case *mein toh aisa tha ki kabhi yeh* down *ho jata toh main hausla badhata tha aur kabhi main* down *ho jata hoon toh yeh bachata hai... toh ek* partner *toh hona chahiya.* And I suggest *ki do log hain toh* best *hain phir jyada* confusion *bhi nahi hai.*

(In our case, if Prabhkiran was feeling low, I would motivate him, if I was low, he would come to my rescue... so, I feel having one partner is definitely a good thing. And, ideally, I feel if there are two founders it is good, it works well.)

Prabhkiran

When you start early, you do not have contacts, you don't have money – it's tough! At every point of time, you will have to prove yourself. But the plus point is that you have more liberty and you can experiment more.

Everyone wants a foolproof plan. But you have to try many different things – some will work, some will not. *Galti se hi aadmi seekhta hai aur aage badhta hai* (You learn from your mistakes). So don't be afraid of mistakes.

You have to go out and you have to act, there is no other way to learn, no other way to be successful.

Ankit Gupta

Dhruv Sogani

LOCHA-E-BUSINESS HO GAYA

Ankit Gupta, Neeraj Agarwal & Dhruv Sogani
(BITS Pilani)
INNOVESE TECHNOLOGIES

Two friends came up with a cool idea and found a way to make it a business. Innovese was a shining star in the startup sky, until interpersonal issues tore the company apart. But there's much you can learn – from their experience.

When I first visited BITS Pilani, I felt a kind of 'magic'.

We alighted at Sawai Madhopur station and took a bus to the campus. Which was literally in the middle of nowhere. Yet, it was bursting with life, colour and energy - hosting the annual cultfest, Oasis.

IIT and BITS have long been mentioned in the same breath - as institutions of excellence. Yet, in some ways, they stand apart.

Pilani students enjoy freedom. They are free to choose their own courses, free to not attend classes, free to just 'be'.

While many take this as a license to 'chill', a few, very few, use this freedom wisely and well. Ankit Gupta, Neeraj Agarwal and Dhruv Sogani are 3 such BITSians.

"I always had this urge to 'do something', so in my third year I started a web-development company along with my batchmate, Neeraj. Later, we invited Dhruv to join us."

Entrepreneurship is a little bit like falling in love. You have a crush on many different business ideas until, one day, you discover The Real Thing. *Phir kya*... you live for that idea and that idea alone.

Something like that happened when Ankit and Neeraj first stumbled on YoCaptcha. *Lekin*, like any great love story, a villain entered the picture. That villain was called 'ego'.

Ek promising startup *ka locha-e-business ho gaya.*

Ultimately, Innovese was sold to German multinational, Gruner+Jahr. Ankit and Dhruv are currently working there while Neeraj has started a new company in the field of analytics and 'big data'.

Love makes your heart strong and your soul flower - even if it does not last 'for ever'. So let love into your heart - love for life, love for work, love for gain, love for growth.

Locha se darne ka nahin - kya!

LOCHA-E-BUSINESS HO GAYA

Ankit Gupta, Neeraj Agarwal & Dhruv Sogani
(BITS Pilani)
INNOVESE TECHNOLOGIES

Ankit Gupta was born and brought up in Jaipur.

"My father is a businessman, while my mother is in government service."

Ankit grew up watching his father struggle in one venture after another, yet he was always fascinated by the idea of starting something of his own. It seemed like the 'cool' thing to do. When he was in Class 5, Ankit got ₹5 from his parents as pocket money during the summer vacations. The young man declared, "I will make hundred rupees out of this five rupee note."

"*Kar ke dikhao*!" said his father.

To please his grandfather, Ankit had got into the habit of reading the newspaper. So he started writing down a summary of the day's news on a sheet of paper and selling carbon copies in his colony.

"See, the thing is, people were not really convinced about buying that but maybe just to encourage me, they would give me 2-3 rupees."

By the end of the month, *Ankit Times – Late City Edition* had earned the princely sum of ₹150.

The turning point for Ankit came when he was in Class 6 and fell in love with computers. A member of the extended family ran a computer-training centre right opposite his house. In the summer vacations, Ankit started helping out – handling the registrations.

“But I also got to use computers. I could see the CD drive and the video playing, I saw what is internet. It was all very exciting!”

The year was 2000 – the PC was a novelty and cybercafés weren’t common in Jaipur. Even the PCs Ankit was using operated on DOS, although Windows ME had been released.

“I have actually worked with 5.25 inch floppies!” recalls Ankit.

The result of this exposure was that, after the vacations, the young man went up to his parents and said, “I want my own PC.”

This was a shocking demand from a 12-year-old at that time. A branded PC with all software loaded cost ₹50,000-70,000. A very big sum for a middle class family. It took 5-6 months of begging and cribbing for Ankit to finally get his ‘dream machine’.

“I nagged my parents until they gave in. But, I think, it is one of the best decisions I took in my life!”

At that time, BSNL had a scheme wherein you could install an internet connection yourself. Which Ankit did.

“Since then, the WWW has been the biggest source of knowledge and motivation in terms of building stuff, of knowing what is happening all around, and writing programs – just for fun.”

One of Ankit’s classmates at St. Anselm’s Pink City Senior Secondary School in Jaipur was Dhruv Sogani.

Dhruv got a PC at home even before Ankit, but he used it for a very different purpose – to play Roadrash!

"I was a computer science student in Class 11 and 12. I had computers as my fifth subject, but that was about it. I am not a programmer," says Dhruv.

Being excellent students, both Ankit and Dhruv joined engineering coaching classes after Class 10 and gave the various entrance exams. A close friendship developed between them at this time.

"We used to chat for hours – What do you want to do when you are in college?... What do you want to do post-college?... What is your philosophy of life... "

At the end of Class 12, Dhruv cleared BITSAT and got admission in Pilani, while Ankit took a one-year drop. The following year, Ankit's scores were good enough to get into the 4-year chemical engineering course but not for the course he really wanted – computer science.

"I was confused and on the verge of taking chemical. But friends like Dhruv who were already at BITS convinced me to go for the 5-year integrated course instead."

The 5-year dual degree is a program at BITS Pilani where a student gets a Master's degree in one of the basic sciences (mathematics, physics, biology or chemistry) along with a BTech. The beauty of the course is that the subject for BTech is allotted on the basis of your performance in the first year.

"I knew Ankit well and I was very sure that he had to be a computer science graduate. So, I pushed him to go for the dual degree and give it a final shot."

The first year at BITS, Ankit was completely focused on studies.

"I knew that I had taken a risk, now I *must* get computer science, else I will be depressed, that is for sure!"

With his eye firmly on the eye of the fish, Ankit got his chosen subject. In the second year of college, he started exploring other aspects of student life.

"Second year in BITS, I think, is the best year because you have less courses and you get to choose your electives."

"My first computer cost ₹70,000 and it was difficult to convince my parents because my previous demands had been board games of 300 or 500 bucks!"

In fact, at BITS, you choose each and everything, right from your teachers to the kind of people you live with, to whether you want to attend classes at all. As attendance is *not* compulsory.

"We were lucky to be part of a student fraternity like BITS Pilani," says Dhruv. "If you are self-motivated, you are surely in the right place!"

Being located in Pilani poses its own set of challenges. Connectivity is an issue, along with so many things you take for granted in metros. Yet, year after year, the students organise and manage the mega cultural festival, Oasis, and a national-level sports meet.

"I was an integral part of Oasis, heading an important department called Publication and Correspondence and interacting with a lot of college students all over India," says Dhruv.

Ankit, on the other hand, came to be known as a designer. He enjoyed working hands-on, creating posters for college events and even User Interface (UI) for websites. By the first semester of his second year at BITS, he decided to convert the free service into a small business.

"I started a design outfit called 'AdShack' with a couple of my batchmates and juniors who were very witty and good with slogans!"

The young team's first client was IYCN (Indian Youth Climate Network) and the assignment involved designing posters for their event, Badlaav 2009. Soon after, they picked up a couple of international clients through a conference held at BITS and made a small amount of money. But, all in all, it was a half-hearted effort.

"The other people with me were not that serious. Besides, I could not see a future in it for myself."

The idea was to 'make it big' and that was just not happening.

At that time, one of the early - and successful - startups on the BITS campus was 'Cube'. One of the co-founders of this company was Neeraj Agarwal - a computer geek and crack programmer. However, the driving force of Cube was a senior called Arvind Singh who graduated in 2009.

"I am a shy guy, always at the back end. I really didn't know how to handle clients!" admits Neeraj.

So what would happen to Cube? As fate would have it, Ankit and Neeraj were randomly chatting on gtalk when there was a 'eureka' moment.

"Why don't we join hands and work together?"*

Both were third-year students, enrolled in the 5-year integrated program. They'd fallen in love with computers at an early age and started writing code. While Neeraj was the superior programmer, Ankit had the design and communication skills.

"We realised that if a designer and developer come together, they can do amazing work."

The first task for the new joint venture was to find a name.

"We googled a lot and then finally thought, 'Let's see what innovation means in different languages.'"

This threw up various spellings and, finally, they settled on 'innovese' because a dotcom name was available. The domain was registered on 8 December 2009.

"The student fraternity at BITS Pilani is *extremely* motivating, it acts as such a good catalyst for people who are self-driven as well."

"As students, we hosted more than 40 websites and did 81 client projects. Totally, we earned some ₹4-5 lakh."

The very first thing the young company did was market itself on social media and to the alumni of BITS Pilani through the website bitsaa.org.

Innovese went 'viral' within the BITS community and quickly picked up a few website and app development projects from within the alumni network. But, one fine day, Innovese got an email from a complete stranger which read as follows:

"Saw you on the internet, your design looks fresh, we would like to get a website done."

The message was from Lalit Kumar, founder of the coaching class, Prime Academy. And he had no connection to BITS. But he was a very good client from whom the team learnt a lot. Initially, Lalit had no idea that he was dealing with a bunch of college kids.

"It was only when I asked to extend a deadline due to exams, that he was intrigued – 'Oh, you are all students?'"

A graduate of IIT Bombay, with no management degree, Lalit had an inspiring story of his own to tell. Starting with just 5 students, he built a multi-crore business spanning 6 centres.

"We had a conversation – he told us how he started up. He also liked our work and was not shy of acknowledging it. That was a positive reinforcement."

Prime Academy paid the young company ₹35,000 for a 15-page website with a forum. All of it was 'profit'. But the team did not go out and blow it all up.

"In Pilani, you can't spend a lot, you don't need pocket money of ₹10,000 a month!"

And what Ankit and Neeraj dreamt about was 'making it big'. They decided to invest ₹17,000 to buy a couple of servers on a lease basis. Now, along with creating websites, the company could offer clients web-hosting services.

"We used to charge ₹3000 a year for website hosting and that substantially increased our earnings!"

The winter vacation gave the team plenty of time to work on projects. By February 2010 - just 3 months in business - Innovese had served 10 clients. Although they were making good money, something was missing.

"By January-end, we were having serious discussions about the future. And, one fine day, we realised - we don't want to be known as a company who makes cheap websites. Let's build something of our own!"

At that time, an application called 'Social Interview' was popular on Facebook. The app posed interesting questions to users about their friends, like, would X like to eat a pizza with or without pepperoni?

"We got kind of inspired by that and by the Slambook concept which was popular in Indian schools."

In February 2010, Ankit and Neeraj began working on a virtual Slambook. The app contained all the usual questions: 'When did you first meet?' 'What do I like about you?' 'My coolest moments', and so on and so forth. The Slambook app went live on Facebook in February 2010 and was a runaway success.

"In a matter of 4 months, we had 85,000 active users and our servers started breaking down."

The app was hosted on the same servers where Innovese

"Instead of taking pocket money, we thought, let's try and invest to develop Slambook a bit more."

"Just because something is new and you are excited about it, doesn't mean others will be excited too... You have to find a way to excite them."

had 30 client websites. The young entrepreneurs decided to take whatever money was coming in through web-development projects and invest it in Slambook.

"By this time, we had started making trips to Delhi, spending on ourselves... but then we thought of putting the money to better use."

The team recoded the application, optimised it, invested in better servers. This helped Slambook grow even faster. In just 8 months, the application had 345,000 users and more than 5 million entries.

"That was our first small success! Interestingly, we even got a buyout offer!!"

Innovese was approached by an FMCG company which was active on social media. They said, "You guys already have 3 lakh users - so why not we rename it and we make it our application."

There were many rounds of discussion, evaluation and negotiation.

"We realised how people think when they are spending money on something. He offered us 50-75 paise per user - the value was in the number of users and not the application itself."

And, of course, the company knew they were dealing with college students.

An offer of a few lakh rupees for a 'buyout' would be attractive enough.

"Actually, it did have that kind of effect on us. We were like, okay, we do so much *mehnat* and end up saving some 30,000-40,000 bucks per head. If we sell out, we will become more famous and also get almost a lakh and a half each!"

It was all very exciting but, ultimately, Ankit and Neeraj decided not to sell.

But, with this process, came the confidence – we *can* build good products. Faith opens doorways, creates pathways. But how does one know *which* path to take?

"Ankit and I discussed many ideas, brainstormed on how we can commercialise them."

These included a carpool app, a professional network ("we used to hate Linkedin at that time") and a custom-website builder ("we actually built that and sold a few copies at Oasis 2010").

Discussion, design and coding went on 24X7. In fact, in August 2010, Innovese became one of the first student-run companies to work from the Technology Business Incubator (TBI) at BITS Pilani. This gave a proper 'office-like' working atmosphere – with zero distraction and blazing-speed internet.

"We used to put all-nighters for days in a row, quite frequently we went to class directly from TBI in the morning!"

The boys even bought a small coffee machine and used to invite batchmates over for late-night *gupshups* and free cuppas. This added to the 'cool factor' of being a student entrepreneur.

The big breakthrough came in the winter of 2010 when results of the mid-sem exam were to be declared. And it happened like this.

"There were examples of seniors whose startup was known for a year, covered by media but ultimately went nowhere. We didn't want that to happen to us!"

"Our batchmates at iAccelerator were using their seed money to develop their product. Our product was ready, so we could start marketing from Day 1."

"We had a web page in college which showed your CGPA before getting the actual CGPA card. All you had to do was enter your ID number."

Not only did people want to see their own marks, they would also enter their friends' ID numbers. Hackers can go one step further – they run a script on the page which generates an Excel sheet of the entire result. To prevent this, the admin put a 'captcha'.

Anyone who uses the internet has definitely come across a captcha. It's that little box where the user has to make sense of a distorted word and enter it. This is to confirm that you are a human being, not a spambot.

The introduction of the captcha may have frustrated some students, but it got Ankit and Neeraj very excited.

"We had a very interesting discussion where we basically said – let's try and break this captcha!"

To do that, they started researching – what is a captcha. Has anyone been able to 'crack' a captcha till date? Suddenly – it clicked.

"We realised that just on this virtual form which is open to only 800 people, we have spent 4 hours solving different captchas. Can you imagine how many captchas are being solved every day on the internet?"

A quick Google search revealed that 280 million captchas were being solved every day on the internet. Multiply that by 2-3 minutes (the average time it takes to solve a captcha) and it adds up to a 'lifetime of attention' on a captcha property per day.

The team also learnt about Recaptcha – a project started

at Carnegie Mellon University by Luis von Ahn to help digitise books. The OCR (Optical Character Recognition) software used to scan books is unable to decipher 30% of words correctly. However, a human being can do the job.

Using the help of millions of people entering captchas every day, Recaptcha was able to decipher blurred words and complete the digitisation of the *New York Times* archives since the year 1851. The company was acquired by Google in the year 2009.

"Recaptcha could translate approximately 10 million words a day, which means there is a huge potential. We thought it should not go waste!"

Mulling over the 'problem' of how to use the captcha as a business idea, there was a eureka moment. Why not use it as an advertising medium? Instead of a random string of alphabets, how about sending Pepsi's brand message and asking the user to type it out?

"Sometimes the captcha is so unclear that you have to type the letters again and again. You even remember the random code AXBY121 on the IRCTC website... So we thought, if it's a brand message, the recall value would be phenomenal!"

Highly charged up, Neeraj and Ankit googled the idea and confirmed that no such application was in existence. Okay – time to get to work!

"We didn't do any sort of architecture or structuring. It was like, okay – let's build this and show the world how cool it is."

That evening Ankit had to travel back to his hometown, Jaipur, but excited by the new idea, Neeraj started

"We learnt that to sell an innovative product, it's best to start at the top – approach the CEO or CTO, not the junior manager."

"We slept on the desk and the floor so many times, because suddenly we would realise that it's already 5 am - we'd been working all night!"

developing the back-end engine. Coding for the first version of YoCaptcha was completed in about 10 days.

"When Ankit came back from Jaipur, I showed him the first mock-up of our product. We then knew it could become a big business."

Around that time, TiE (The Indus Entrepreneurs) was holding its annual conference in Delhi. The young men decided to attend the event and get some feedback on YoCaptcha.

The product was not that good looking, more like a student project. While it was appreciated as a 'great idea', there were also many questions.

"It actually made us realise that just developing a product is not enough..."

You might be 'cool' in your college, your professors may think you are doing something great. But the ground reality is, you have to think of expenses, EBIDTA*, business plan and so on.

"At that time, I used to have shoulder-length hair and a beard - I was a proper college brat," recalls Ankit. "I was like - fuck all that - we are going to revolutionise the advertising industry!"

However, on returning to Pilani, the young man realised that a lot of things needed to be done.

"In my lifetime in college, I had seen so many ideas which were lost because people didn't know how to actually bring it to the market."

---

* EBITDA = Earnings Before Interest, Taxes, Depreciation and Amortisation.

"We also participated in a lot of business-plan competitions such as Tata NEN First Dot, where we were selected among the Top 30."

By this time, the team had a working 'demo'. They were running a pilot program with a couple of websites and 2-3 dummy advertisers.

"This blog called 'Youth *ki Awaaz'* is owned by Anshul Tiwari, whom we met at the TiE conference. We requested him to let us try out YoCaptcha on the site."

It was a phase of learning, growth and maturing. The quality of thought and discussion started changing. From something 'cool' and fun, the team began to think of a 'future' as entrepreneurs.

"We were still doing many different things at the same time. The web development, hosting Slambook and, of course – studies!"

While YoCaptcha was not yet generating revenue, Innovese had around 120 clients from Europe, US and India, while Slambook had its 300,000-plus users. Yet, instinctively, the team felt it had to focus on YoCaptcha.

"We didn't kill off Slambook... it kind of died a natural death."

This was partly because the team shifted its focus to YoCaptcha – and partly because of external factors. Every time Facebook updated its developer APIs, the team would have to rejig the application so that it continued to work.

"At some point, we lost interest in updating the app and many of the features stopped working."

At that time, the Slambook page boasted 37,000 'likes'.

"Our friends were in good jobs by then... taking holidays in Goa. While we were worrying about the next month's electricity bill!"

"People no longer doubt what we are capable of. And yes, parents feel *ki bande jo kar rahe hain, theek kar rahe hain.*"

Overnight, Facebook changed its policy and the counter was reset to 'zero'.

"This really pissed us off... we wrote a couple of mails to Facebook but they didn't care - we were nobody, we gave up."

By the end of the fourth year, Ankit was no longer a topper - but managing. Studying just before the exams, he was able to 'maintain' a CGPA above 8 throughout his college life.

"Actually, I could manage my studies along with the business but I had lost interest in academics. So I ended up with a D in a couple of subjects and decided it's okay!"

Being a 9 pointer in the first and second year helped 'average' out the 4.3 CGPA Ankit scored in his third year.

"I kind of tricked my parents because, see, the thing is, in a report card you always get a cumulative grade."

Grades reflect what the world thinks of you. What really matters is what *you* think of yourself.

In June 2011, Ankit and Neeraj went for Practice School - a 6-month compulsory internship for BITS students in the final year. While Ankit interned with Bravo Lucy in Hyderabad, Neeraj was with Opera Solutions in Noida. What Innovese really needed at this point was a marketing brain.

"In August 2011, we asked Dhruv to come on board and work on business development along with Ankit."

Dhruv had taken a semester break and gone to Germany for an internship with BMW. Hence, he had another 6 months before he could graduate from BITS. Instead of enrolling for classes, he opted for a 'thesis' and started working with an automotive consulting company in Gurgaon.

"Although my first love is auto, I was excited by the concept of YoCaptcha. Also, I knew Ankit since our schooldays, so I agreed to join them."

Soon after, the team learnt about iAccelerator at IIM Ahmedabad – a 3-month mentorship program for early-stage internet startups. They'd just missed the deadline but put fight and sent in the application. The effort paid off. Innovese was one of the 9 startups selected for the year 2010-11.

There was one small problem – Neeraj and Ankit had to complete their internships, Dhruv had to submit his thesis.

They requested Pranay Gupta, Joint CEO of IIMA CIIE (Centre for Innovation, Incubation and Entrepreneurship), "Please allow us to join after one month!"

An exception was made for the young entrepreneurs – they joined the program a month late, determined to make the best of it. It was back to working from a hostel room, up to 20 hours at a stretch.

"Sometimes it was necessary to go out and take fresh air!"

It was placement season at BITS Pilani and Neeraj received interview calls from companies like Epic, Pocket Gems and McKinsey. He refused them all. As for Ankit – he did not even register for placement. Neither did he want to return to campus to attend classes.

As luck would have it, Ankit's Practice School employer got selected for the same iAccelerator program. The founders of Framebench* were batchmates from BITS and agreed to let Ankit do a 'fake' internship – in order to meet his academic requirements.

"That way I continued working on my own product and ultimately I got an 'A' in my report card (smiles)."

The iAccelerator experience helped in many, many ways.

* Framebench was earlier known as Anaya Labs. It was founded by Rohit Agarwal and Vineet Markan from BITS Pilani.

"People put in a lot of effort in being a 'good guy' in a big company. If you put the same amount of force in your startup, you will do more and better work!"

Unlike other startups in the program, the Innovese product was ready to roll. So what the team did was figure out the dynamics of running a business.

"First of all, we realised that we are in the advertising media industry. So, we have to understand how this industry works."

What is an advertising agency? Media buying agency? How do clients behave?... And what is the right way to approach them? Can you approach a company like Pepsi directly or do you go through their agency?

"We were not aware of any of these things!"

What's more, the iAccelerator program arranged for interactions with industry experts such as Alok Kejriwal (contests2win), Gaurav Sharma (media2win), Manish Dalal (Verisign) and Amit Somani (MakeMyTrip).

"By the end of the program, we knew how to talk with the 'tools of the trade' like CPM, CTR and ROI*."

As part of the iAccelerator program, every startup receives a seed fund investment of ₹5 lakh. 50% of this money comes from CIIE and 50% from angel investors. Anuj Pulstya and Maneesh Bhandari were the angels who invested in Innovese.

Ventures running as sole proprietorships and partnerships also receive help with incorporation. Thus, Innovese became a private limited company.

---

* CPM = Cost Per Thousand (M) Impressions, ROI = Return on Investment, CTR = Click Through Rate.

iAccelerator concluded on 27 January 2012. In February, the team decided to relocate to Delhi.

"One of our investors (Anuj) had an office space in Rajendra Nagar which he allowed us to use without paying market rent."

A great co-working space is more than a collection of tables and chairs – it is a meeting of minds. And that's exactly what happened at Rajendra Nagar. Framebench and Innovese shared the office with Anuj Pulstya and his wife, Neeru Sharma.

"Anuj and Neeru became an important support system for us. We spent numerous evenings discussing the future of Innovese!"

The atmosphere was charged with hopes and dreams. The entry time to office was 10 am but there was no exit time. Neeraj would commute from his home in Ghaziabad, Ankit and Dhruv rented a flat nearby. But, often, they had no energy to walk across and simply dozed off in the office.

This was a new phase for the company, of pitching the product to clients. Innovese had to capture two sets of stakeholders – advertisers who would pay to display their brand message and websites which had enough traffic to display a large number of captchas. Getting a meeting was the first challenge.

"We can tell you all the different sorts of ways we approached companies – a lot of it was simply cold calling!"

The first big website to sign on was Ibibo.com, followed by Zapak, Way2sms and the entire Jagran group. The toughest nut to crack was *The Times of India* (TOI).

"I personally would have met close to 10-12 people within *The Times of India* group, from the assistant manager to the CTO and even the CEO."

It took 4 months to 'close the deal' and that too, on their terms. *The Times of India* management stated up front that whenever it came across an innovation, the in-house R&D team would try to duplicate it.

"We cannot sign an agreement that we won't develop a competing product," they said.

The young entrepreneurs agreed – for two reasons. Firstly, they badly wanted to be on *The Times of India* platform. And secondly, they were pretty sure the company would not be able to reverse-engineer YoCaptcha.

"Our proposition was very attractive – we will get advertisers and do a revenue share with your website. So you make money with zero effort."

The next task was finding advertisers. And this was not easy either. Although there was a lot of interest in the idea, there were also a lot of doubts and questions.

"We used to approach advertising agencies as well as large clients like HUL and P&G."

But, from February to May, no client committed even a single rupee of business. Hence, at the same time, the team also made several pitches to investors. None of them yielded funds, but there were other benefits. A pitch to Mumbai Angels, for example, got Ravi Kiran interested in the project.

"Ravi Kiran is an advertising veteran, he became our mentor."

In June 2012, Innovese got its first big breakthrough. A release order from Reliance Industries. And from then on, there was no looking back. Clients such as HUL, Star World, Axis Bank and State Bank of India followed.

"We did campaigns for as little as ₹25,000-30,000 and as much as ₹5-6 lakh for a period of 1 week."

This revenue was shared between Innovese and a publisher, say, *The Times of India,* on a 60:40 basis.

Once money started coming in, the tension eased. However, there was still a bit of a cash-flow problem. Advertising agencies pay 60 to 90 days after completion of a campaign.

"By this time, we had exhausted the ₹5 lakh from

iAccelerator. So we had to put in some amount of personal funds."

The struggle to get business was one side of the story and it has a happy ending. The struggle to keep the founders together is another side of the story and that ended badly. Cracks developed in the once-cohesive team after shifting to Delhi.

Neeraj stopped coming to the Rajendra Nagar office - he preferred to work virtually, via phone calls and emails. This hit the morale of the team.

"We felt Neeraj started slacking off, as the business was not rolling. He was the key programmer, his absence hit us badly."

Neeraj had a genuine problem - he had to attend office daily. His Practice School (PS) was with Opera Solutions in Noida and this was not college, which you could simply bunk.

"I had even offered to contribute my stipend to the company account. But somehow... we had differences... things were no longer the same."

A startup is like a baby - it needs constant nurturing and attention. If the mother is distracted, the baby starts wailing. When the founder is distracted, the startup starts ailing.

Ankit hoped that things would 'return to normal' when Neeraj joined the company full-time in May, after completing his PS. But by that time, Neeraj had decided to part ways. They did try to talk it out, sort it out, work it out. *Nahin hua*.

In June 2012, Neeraj formally quit Innovese via sms. He had accepted a lucrative job offered by Opera Solutions.

After Neeraj left, Ankit had to shift his focus away from marketing, to the technology aspect of the business. Captcha is a critical feature on any website - if it doesn't work, the web form will not get submitted.

"At one point, we were doing 250 captchas a second - that was a technical challenge!"

On the selling front, Dhruv was supported by some interns. While the interns did not actually meet clients, they helped to develop the business case, do background research and make presentations. The interns were mostly from Delhi University though one came all the way from Hyderabad.

"The guy was so keen to work with us, he said, 'Don't worry, I will come down at my own expense. Just pay me a small monthly stipend!'"

Clients constantly want something 'new', hence, over time, Innovese developed an interactive captcha. Instead of typing a text message, the user would have to do something interesting like drag the opener over a Pepsi bottle.

"We had to constantly innovate to keep the advertisers excited!"

Subsequently, Innovese came up with a survey-based captcha. To protect the IP behind this novel idea, they even applied for a PDC (Patent Data Capture) from the Indian Patent Office.

Another proud moment was Ankit winning the Global Student Entrepreneur Award from India (North) in November 2012. This qualified him to attend an event hosted at the New York Stock Exchange for the Global Finals. While he did not win, it was a great learning experience.

"I got to know how international business experts see ideas, and got valuable feedback from them."

In its first year of operations - ending 31 March 2013 - YoCaptcha billed ₹30 lakh in revenue.

Eyeing more business, Innovese entered into an alliance with the digital advertising platform, Network Play. The company had a sales team which could help YoCaptcha reach out to more advertisers. The two entities agreed to work together on a 'revenue sharing' basis.

"We accompanied the team for some of the meetings and pitches. Then we got introduced to the CEO, Rammohan

Sundaram, who was excited about YoCaptcha – the team and how we built the product."

That's when the first conversation about a 'buyout' started happening.

Originally a startup, Network Play was acquired by German publisher Gruner and Jahr (G+J) of the Bertelsmann group in March 2012. Like all big publishers, the company was scrambling to adapt to the digital age. YoCaptcha was a good fit and a great opportunity.

"The conversation went on for 3 months and in June we closed it informally."

Before taking a decision, Ankit and Dhruv did seek advice from their seed investors and from Pranay Gupta who had been the coordinator of the iAccelerator program and a mentor since.

"At one level, we did think – we can continue on our own. But we also felt that Gruner + Jahr can do justice to the product, take it much further."

The deal was concluded in September 2013. Post-merger, Ankit became Head of Technology at Network Play while Dhruv is Head of Business Development.

"At present, we are enjoying our roles and happy to continue here."

But, somewhere, there is the question 'what if'. What if Innovese had been a startup in Silicon Valley?

"Definitely, your worth is much more in the US – small companies get acquired for much higher valuations."

And, what if the team had stuck together through thick and thin?

"We could have definitely raised money from investors... grown the company ourselves!"

While Neeraj 'left' the company, on paper he was still a major shareholder. And this was a grave concern for potential investors. Ankit and Dhruv spent many sleepless nights – reading the contracts and books on company law. There was no easy way out.

"We learnt a lesson about how important 'a team' is and what serious and dangerous hassles you can have even if one member quits."

Things fall apart - in love, in war, in business. While nobody made big money by selling out, it gave the young entrepreneurs an exit. A chance to wipe the slate clean and start again.

Ankit's parents are definitely proud of his achievements. Yes, along the way, they could never really 'understand' *ki yeh kar kya raha hai* (what the hell is our son doing?)

Dhruv's parents were fairly liberal but they still worried when they saw him struggling.

"I have an elder cousin who runs a successful software company - he is my role model and a constant source of inspiration."

Neeraj came from a business family background so there were no parental issues - they were extremely supportive. And, overall, being a student entrepreneur was a great experience.

"It's delightful to be able to pay your own college fees and, most of all, it made me a workaholic... I mean, a person who keeps working until he succeeds!"

Neeraj is currently working on a new venture called Algoscale - a startup in the domain of big-data and predictive analytics.

You stumble, you fall, you get up and start walking again. But you've got to begin *somewhere*. That somewhere could be your very own hostel room.

Ek simple *sa sawaal hai* - are you gonna keep sitting on your butt or actually do something?

ADVICE TO YOUNG ENTREPRENEURS

We definitely advise starting a venture in college because in those years you have the maximum amount of time and energy to work on something 'crazy'.

Second thing is, you don't have that many responsibilities on your shoulders and you have lot of good people around you who are willing to help – your peers, advisors and mentors.

Being a campus startup gives you a head start. We had time to revisit the product again and again without pressure of sales. In those two years, I was paying ₹1000 as my hostel fee for 6 months. Whereas, once you graduate, you have to pay ₹10,000 per month to share a flat.

So starting early, starting in campus is actually a smart thing to do – go for it!

Ankit

If, at 21-22, you have taken the decision to start up, you have shown a hint of maturity. You are consciously taking a decision of not taking up a job.

You have had a flash of genius and found something you can passionately work on. When times are tough, do not think of yourself as a failure or think about failure. Do not think about giving up.

If you are convinced yourself, only then you can convince your parents. Be very frank with them and be firm about your decision.

I would also advise college startups to sign a 'co-founder agreement'. This would be very useful in case one of the founders decides to suddenly opt out of the company due to family pressure or lure of placements.

Dhruv

One of the things I have seen in myself and the people around me – if you are not self-driven about something, you will give up very easily.

Whatever you are planning, you must enjoy it, no matter if there is a lot of criticism around it or you are struggling with it.

Your single biggest strength is belief in what you are doing, the desire to take a particular idea to the level where me, myself and the larger society is going to be proud of it.

There is a lot of glamour around startups today... it's easy to create an app, get written about and start feeling, 'I have made it!' You are 'up in the air' – which is great – but at some point you have to become grounded and practical... you have to build a sustainable business.

Neeraj

College time is the best time to experiment with your life. Make full use of any opportunity in terms of internship and be open to learning as much as possible.

You can use this time to work on your business plan, prepare a demo or a MVP (Minimum Viable Product). And don't worry about maintaining a high CGPA but just a decent CGPA as a fallback option.

Don't take all courses lightly, some of them are really good and can help you in the startup as well.

AWARA PAAGAL DEEWANA

Rupesh Shah (IET, Alwar)
INOPEN TECHNOLOGIES

An internship at IIT Bombay changed the course of Rupesh Shah's life. A self-taught programmer, marketer and 'people person', his company, InOpen Technologies, now teaches computer science to over 5 lakh schoolchildren.

Lakhs of students appear for IIT JEE but only a few thousand make it. Those who do not, fall in the eyes of family and friends.

At age 17 or 18, you start considering yourself a 'failure'.

Rupesh Shah was one such student - he not only failed to enter IIT, he failed his Class 12 board exams. He failed to enter any engineering college on merit and then, he went on to fail in the first year university exam.

Failure *bhi usse tang aakar boli* - "*Jao, koi aur* girlfriend *dhoondo!*"

That new 'girlfriend' was open-source software - a passion, an obsession, *ek jee jaan wali mohabbat*. A wonderful new world opened, life *ne liya* U-turn.

Rupesh joined IIT Bombay as an intern. Sitting in a small cubicle in the computer laboratory, he felt blessed to simply 'be there'.

"For 4 months, I worked 16–18 hours a day. Because I had got this chance to prove myself!"

This was Rupesh's first brush with 'success'. He went on to start one company (and fail), then start another company (and almost fail).

After 5 years in existence, InOpen Technologies has finally moved on from thin ice to firm ground. The company imparts computer science education to over 5 lakh students in 200 schools across India, in the US and Japan.

Pyaar kiya to darna kya, fail *huye to marna kya.*

Find a new 'girlfriend', a reason to live for, a reason to smile.

AWARA PAAGAL DEEWANA

Rupesh Shah (IET, Alwar)
INOPEN TECHNOLOGIES

Rupesh Kumar Shah was born in Siliguri, a small town near Darjeeling.

"My father is a timber merchant, I grew up seeing my dad and uncle sell wood and run a saw mill. There used to be wood and sawdust all around our house!"

It was a middle-income Marwari family, where the trend was to join dad in business after college. During vacations, Rupesh did go to the office and help with invoices. But he seemed to lack the '*bania*' gene.

"Once, I advised a customer to go for plastic instead of wood because I thought it would be more cost-effective."

When the manager narrated this incident to Rupesh's father, he shook his head in disbelief. *Iss ladke se* business *nahin hone wala,* better he aim for IIT. Like every other aspirant, Rupesh joined Bansal Classes in Kota to prepare for JEE.

But things did not go as planned.

"Somewhere, I went astray and did not clear IIT. On top of that, I even failed my Class 12 board exam."

It was a big shock – from 90% in Class 10 to a compartment in physics. Rupesh reappeared for the examination but those 3 months were long and agonising.

"That was the most depressing part of my life. Only my sister encouraged me, persuaded me not to give up."

In fact, Rupesh had secured admission in the marine engineering course. But his father was dead against it – *nahin karne diya.* Now what?

"I could not even return to Siliguri and face my classmates who had stayed back and got very good results."

Finally, Rupesh secured admission in a private engineering college at Alwar (Rajasthan) by paying a donation of ₹50,000. Initially, it was difficult for him to adjust in college because he constantly felt – 'I could have done better'. In this state of mind, he flunked the first-year university examination.

"Somehow, I cleared my supplementary."

At this low point in life, Rupesh saw a ray of hope in the form of open source. He developed a fascination for Linux and spent hours in the computer lab trying to understand what could be done with it.

"Linux is a great platform but too geeky for the layman. I felt there was a need for a hybrid operating system which could be used by newbies."

Since no such program was available, Rupesh decided to build one himself. But first, he wanted to get some experience, do an internship. Sitting in the canteen one day, he overheard a senior whose brother's friends had done internship in IIT Bombay.

"At that moment, I made up my mind – I have to be at IIT Bombay."

Rupesh looked up the telephone number of IITB on the internet and started cold calling various professors. After one and a half months of effort, he managed to get the head of the computer science department, Professor Phatak, on the line. The professor was none too pleased.

"Do not disturb me again," was his curt response.

But Rupesh was not one to take 'no' easily. He kept sending mails and calling the professor, explaining what his open-source project was about. And that it *could* be done. How exactly, he didn't know but he would make it happen.

"I bugged Professor Phatak to the extent that he finally gave up and allowed me to intern for 3 months."

In fact, Rupesh convinced him to let 3 of his friends also join the project. Professor Shridhar from the computer science department arranged for hostel accommodation and agreed to be his mentor. As did Venkatesh Hariharan, who was then the head of 'Red Hat' in India.

"It was more like they gave some broad guidelines – beyond that you are on your own!"

The internship started in July 2005 and Rupesh threw his heart and soul into it. For 4 months, he used to code for 12–14 hours at a stretch, every day, including Sundays. The Affordable Solutions Lab at IIT Bombay was like a temple and Rupesh, its most ardent devotee.

IIT *mein* entry *ka nasha toh tha hi, saath hi apne ko* prove *karne ka josh.*

At the end of 4 months, Rupesh and team succeeded in creating 'Intux OS' – a user-friendly 'Windows style' Linux operating system. Professor Phatak and Professor Shridhar were both very happy – things were finally looking up! But all of a sudden, life threw up a whole new challenge.

"My mother was diagnosed with breast cancer and was admitted to Raheja Hospital. I put all my work on hold to focus on her treatment."

Life now revolved around radiation, chemotherapy and surgery. After a delicate operation, she miraculously recovered from third-stage cancer.

"My sister Mittu is a very strong person who deserves all the credit for getting our mother the best treatment possible."

"I did not know what is a company, what is 'private limited'. I just signed wherever I was told to. That was my big mistake."

"If you do good work, you can always repeat yourself and succeed again. I realised this very early."

Rupesh returned to IIT to complete the project and launched it in mid-2006. Over the next few months, 'Intux' was downloaded by over 100,000 users. Being open source, the program was free, so there was no money to be made. But it was indeed a source of pride and joy.

The 3-month intership at IIT had been 'extended' indefinitely. In fact, in the fifth, sixth and seventh semesters, Rupesh's attendance in college was 0.0%.

"Luckily, my college chairman was supportive and asked the department heads to accommodate me. I somehow managed to just pass my exams."

In the last month of college, Rupesh started a training company in partnership with his college chairman. 3 of his classmates joined as well. The venture was to train engineering graduates on open-source software.

"I realised that to make Intux successful, we need to increase the awareness of Linux itself."

The venture took off immediately - within 6 months, the company-trained 6000 students and even secured a contract from the Indian Air Force. The team conducted 7-day, 14-day and 30-day training sessions all over Rajasthan, Mumbai and Delhi.

At the end of 6 months, the company's revenues had crossed ₹60 lakh but, to his surprise, Rupesh learnt that his cheques were bouncing.

"I came to know that the company was running on ad-hoc basis. Also, my stake was not 49% as promised but merely 20%."

With blind faith, Rupesh had signed on empty ROC*

* A private limited company must be registered with the ROC (Registar of Companies).

forms. With great difficulty, the young man confronted the college chairman. He promised to re-draft the agreement and 'start afresh'. But he didn't keep that commitment. Rupesh decided to just 'walk away' without asking for his dues or share.

"I told my team that I don't see a future and I can no more continue. The most satisfying part was that my entire team too walked away with me."

That same night Rupesh landed in Mumbai with two of his colleagues – Mukul and Ruchi. The city had a special place in his heart – it was full of possibilities.

"I felt that I can reinvent myself... I can do something awesome in this city."

But first, there were practical realities to face. For 45 days, Rupesh stayed in a shady hotel near Vihar Lake for ₹400 a day. Funds were slowly getting exhausted.

"One fine day, I was left with no money to even have lunch. But, somehow, I never asked my Dad for money!"

The silver lining to this cloud was that Rupesh had reconnected with Professor Shridhar. And found a great new idea to work on.

The professor had a passion for education technology and had developed a model computer science curriculum. Being an academic, his plan was to simply publish it on the internet for anyone to use. But the 'business gene' in Rupesh quickly spotted a big opportunity – working with schools.

"Professor Shridhar liked the idea and let me work from the meeting room in his office. That was like a big thing for me, *ki main* IIT *mein kaam kar raha hoon*!"

Within a month, Rupesh was meeting with schools across Mumbai to understand ground realities. Unlike history, geography or mathematics, computer science is a relatively new subject. Hence, teaching methods and material were still evolving. But, no doubt, *something* was lacking.

"The unique thing about our curriculum was the focus on critical thinking."

"I want to fundamentally change the way technology is taught in this country."

Thinking big and bold, Rupesh proposed to set up a company, with Professor Shridhar as a co-founder. The good professor was reluctant – the world of business was alien to him. But the young man's passion and commitment was infectious.

"Let's do it!" he said.

To incorporate the company, you need to employ a chartered accountant. Rupesh turned to Justdial and located a CA – Ashutosh Srivastava – right outside the IIT gate. He met the gentleman and explained his vision and mission.

"I also told Ashutosh *ki abhi hamare paas paise nahin hai.* But when I have money, I will definitely pay you."

The CA agree to work on the basis of trust. In fact, he went a step further and offered the use of half his office to the young entrepreneur. Rupesh and his 4 team members gladly accepted. 'InOpen Technologies' was incorporated on 30 September 2009, with Rupesh and Professor Sridhar as co-founders.

"I am indebted to Ashutosh for his help in everything, right from accounts to nitty gritties of company formation."

While Rupesh was responsible for the day-to-day running of the company, Professor Sridhar came on board as a non-executive director.

Side by side, Rupesh had been putting up a fight to get incubated by SINE (Society for Innovation and Entrepreneurship) at IIT Bombay.

"When I tried for incubation, they told me you have to submit a business plan. At that time I had no idea *yeh kya hota hai*!"

Thinking the more detailed the better, Rupesh submitted a 78-page business plan. The external reviewer sent it back with a message: "I will see your plan only if you make it 11 pages, including the thank you and introduction."

After 4 rounds of iterations, Rupesh managed to pare down his plan to the bare minimum and resubmit it. Industry veterans, including Anand Deshpande and Dr Shridhar Shukla (Persistent Systems) and Shantanu Prakash (Educomp), reviewed the plan.

"I must have given at least 15 interviews before they finally gave the green signal!"

InOpen Technologies joined the IIT Bombay incubator on 23 November 2009.

A business model was slowly taking shape. InOpen offered two models to schools – it would provide the content as well as a teacher, or it would train the existing teachers. The big challenge was finding a school to start the pilot project.

"The IIT association gave us a lot of credibility but trustees and principals had a valid concern – what if we start and you go out of business tomorrow?"

It takes time and patience to convince a school to make any kind of change.

The first school to implement InOpen's 'Computer Masti' curriculum was the Sri Sri Ravishankar Vidyamandir (SSRVM) in Mulund, followed by Borivili. Both the principal, Miss Neena, and the staff-in-charge, Mrs Bageshri, were extremely cooperative.

"We had some minor issues but were able to overcome them quickly. We started with Classes 1 to 3 and got a very positive response."

What's more, the school paid in advance for one quarter – resulting in a billing of ₹4 lakh. However, to build a team

"Incubation support from IIT Bombay gave me this feeling that I can do anything, I can change the world!"

"We found that schools were willing to pay anywhere between ₹300-₹1000 per student."

with expertise in marketing as well as academics, it would not be enough.

"Apart from salaries, printing of books was a major expense - almost 25% of our budget."

The project needed an angel investor and that angel with wings of faith was Professor Sridhar himself. He burrowed into his life savings and wrote out 4 cheques of ₹5 lakh each to the company. Additionally, Rupesh borrowed around ₹3 lakh from friends.

"As part of our incubation at SINE, we also received a soft loan of ₹15 lakh at 5% interest per annum."

Money is important, but not everything is available for sale. The intellectual input from IIT Bombay faculty - in particular, Professor Sridhar, Professor Farida and Professor Malti - was one such priceless asset.

"They are all gurus in computer science who selflessly supported the project. For a startup to get such talent would otherwise be impossible!"

The InOpen curriculum covers all aspects of CS from computer fundamentals to programming, publishing, internet safety and ethics. But, unlike the usual 'textbook' style, the InOpen curriculum takes a narrative approach.

"There are 3 characters - Tejas, Jyoti and Moiz - who interact with each other and explain concepts. We call it as dialogue-format guided enquiry method."

Computer science is also a tool to create the habit of step-wise thinking.

"Every activity can be broken into smaller activities. And this is the way we want kids to start thinking right from Class 2 or Class 3."

To introduce educationists to this new method of teaching, InOpen adopted an out-of-the-box idea. From the very first year, Rupesh decided to organise a conference for school principals. The topic was Computer Science Research and the venue was IIT Bombay campus itself.

"The first year we managed to get only 7 principals but that set the trend. Now, every year we do many such events."

By March 2010, InOpen had revenues of ₹10 lakh and a loss of ₹16 lakh. The company was working with 8 schools, providing them a printed textbook, an open-source software bundle and teacher training. What's more, the curriculum was customised depending on the level of the students.

"Our vision was that this content should not be limited to elite schools."

Thus, even as the 'Computer Masti' syllabus was used by Jamnabai Narsee School in Juhu, it was also adopted by schools in the slums of Dharavi and Thane. To expand the reach of the program, InOpen took the bold step of converting the content into 8 regional languages and two foreign languages.

"That was a costly project but it was important as we wanted to reach maximum number of students!"

This massive exercise was made possible with the help of a term loan from the State Bank of India under CGTMSE*. Under this scheme, a loan of up to ₹2 crore can be disbursed by the concerned officer, if convinced about the viability of a project. What's more, it is an unsecured loan – no collateral required.

"It took us 4 months but finally, in August 2010, we received ₹50 lakh under the CGTSME scheme. This helped us grow at a tremendous pace."

By March 2011, InOpen's revenue team was 23-strong and revenues had jumped to ₹72 lakh, though the company was still in the red. But Rupesh remained unperturbed.

---

* A scheme from Credit Guarantee Fund Trust for Micro and Small Enterprises (CGTMSE) under which banks can lend up to ₹2 crore to an SME without collateral.

"I believe parents' opinions will change with time. Parents *ko shuru mein thoda sa* ignore *karo, baad mai samajh jayenge*."

"I knew that when you grow quickly, you may not make profit immediately. A loss of ₹8-10 lakh is perfectly fine."

In the summer of 2011, Aditya Natarajan from the VC firm Ventureast visited SINE and was impressed by the size and scale of InOpen's operations. At that time, the company was catering to 40,000 students in 52 schools - but there was scope to do so much more!

Ventureast agreed to invest $500,000 in seed money to accelerate the growth of the young company. Dr Shridhar Shukla (then COO of Persistent Systems) joined the InOpen board.

"From Day 1, the company was operating in a transparent and structured manner. That made it easier to get the funds."

In March 2012, InOpen crossed a turnover of ₹2.3 crore with a profit of ₹13 lakh. Things were going well, talks were underway to raise the next round of funds. A deal was clinched with a global education company - an investment of ₹40 crore as well as a strategic partnership.

"We had completed the formalities and were just waiting for money to hit the bank. But that never happened!"

On 31 December 2012, InOpen received a high-voltage shock. The investor who was to put in $8 million shut down its India operations - the merger was off. The trouble was, InOpen had already 'spent' the money, expanded the staff, printed materials. Now the company simply had no cash.

"To describe the situation, we had 44 employees and just ₹2000 in the bank!"

Would the company survive? That was the burning question.

"At that moment, I did not have a single thought about the future. I focused only on the present."

When a house is on fire, people run to the exit. But the InOpen team stayed on to fight - down to the last man standing. Employees pooled in their savings, even borrowed from friends. Salaries were delayed by 3 months, but *log juday rahe, lagey rahe*.

"I am blessed to have such a team, a team that believed in me and what we had set out to do."

Faith can move mountains and, in this case, it moved InOpen's board members to loosen their purse strings. A soft loan was extended to the company, to tide over the crisis. Similarly, many customers agreed to pay in advance for the entire year. A few even lent their own money in the form of debt.

"Those 4-5 months were really difficult, I used to be very tense!"

In November 2013, InOpen *ke achhe din aa gaye*. The company received a strategic investment from the Japanese education company - Benesse Holdings. The valuation was 5 times higher than what it was 24 months earlier. And this was highly unusual.

"Most startups get a valuation based on revenue multiples. In our case, the valuation comes from IP (Intellectual Property)."

To create fun, interactive material, InOpen had embraced 'Scratch', a visual programming language developed by MIT's Media Lab. Professor Mitchel Resnick invited Rupesh to come to Boston and talk about his work. This was a very exciting moment for the young entrepreneur.

"Our product was highly appreciated and even referred to as the 'best CS education solution' in the world!" by Professor Resnick and his team."

The unofficial MIT endorsement gave Rupesh the confidence to take a bold step. A pilot program using Computer Masti syllabus in 7 Silicon Valley schools, in partnership with Benesse. The material was redesigned as it was not to be in book-form but for an iPad.

"I have been inspired by people like Alexis Ohanian, Narayana Murthy, Hrithik Roshan and Richard Branson (my HERO)."

InOpen also began collaborating with state education departments. The first to adopt Computer Masti was Assam - approximately 4 lakh students of government schools are now learning computer science in this way.

"We are also doing projects with the government in Bihar, Goa and Maharashtra."

By March 2014, InOpen was working with over 350 schools and had achieved sales of ₹3.6 crore. The company started operations in Jaipur and Hyderabad and continued to expand in Mumbai.

"On the academic side, we now have PhDs, instructional designers, masters in psychology. We recently hired someone who worked with Google!"

Rupesh is a strong believer in the power of interns and internship. In the last 5 years, InOpen has had more than 30 interns.

"When I hired the first IITian, I was thrilled. I love my interns and promote internship in our organisation."

And no matter how far InOpen may have come, Rupesh cannot forget its humble roots. Like the 1 BHK flat where he lived for many months with 12 of his initial colleagues. And bonded with each other deeply.

"Out of 8 college mates who joined me, 5 are still with the company and also own shares."

Over the last year, Rupesh has refused two 'acquisition offers'. In fact, InOpen bought back the 1% stake given to IIT as per the terms of incubation. Thus earning the institute a handsome return. What's more, among all the incubatees at SINE, InOpen turned profitable in the shortest period of time.

The company's future plans include entering the B2C

segment through digital books and partnerships with universities, as well as with Khan Academy.

"Our aim is to become a global face in teaching computer science."

And to even go beyond. InOpen has acquired a science syllabus from the Homi Bhabha Centre for Science Education called 'Small Science'. The team will work on it, fine-tune it and, possibly, change the way science is taught.

"The idea is to help students develop critical-thinking skills – no matter what the subject."

In his own quest to learn and grow, Rupesh has been pursuing an executive MBA in business analytics from IIM Calcutta. The course has helped in understanding numbers and 'patterns'.

"When I joined the course, I was just 24, making me the youngest in the batch!"

As for his family, Rupesh says they are finally 'happy'. Especially when they see his work being recognised, featured in newspapers.

"Parents will always want you to live a normal life, they will want you to not struggle," he shrugs.

It's your choice, whether to give in or hang in there. And the same, he says, applies to the biggest decision of all – marriage. Coming from a Marwari family, there is immense pressure on Rupesh to 'settle down'.

But when you have felt great passion, you want to feel it in every area of your life. Settling for less is not an option.

"Right now... I am a little burnt out. I really need a break!"

But this too shall pass. The high and the low, the ebb and the flow.

"Numerous times I was on the verge of giving up. I somehow managed to survive, to keep faith."

Stillness within the centre of a storm. In the darkness of night, hope of dawn. Failure teaches you many lessons, the biggest lesson – stay calm, move on.

ADVICE TO YOUNG ENTREPRENEURS

Enthusiasm and passion are the only keys to success. An enthusiastic human being with good intent somehow manages to do good and land on the correct path.

When I started in my college, I didn't know that a word called startup existed and till date I get the spelling of entrepreneurship wrong.

We all face problems but problems have a common pattern. A 'big' problem of the past becomes ordinary in the present. Similarly, the 'big' problem today will become ordinary issue. Just hang on!

I failed many times and faced many challenges. I am no superman but I just managed to stick with my goals. My failures taught me one thing – that I don't have anything to lose from this point but only gain.

Perseverance matters the most. I love my failures and, in a true sense, made them my pillars of support.

Doing MBA from an obscure college, joining ordinary jobs and switching jobs are common traits among students today. You can do much much better! But first, you must believe in yourself.

Identify what you like and focus on that even while you are a student.

Your objective should not be, 'I want to work for myself.' Instead you should first work and if the work needs to be expanded, then you start a company.

Chahe kitne bhi mistakes *karo. Log kuch bhi bole*, just keep doing it.

When you are enthusiastic about something or passionate about something, you somehow reach there.

REBELS WITH A CAUSE

These mavericks strayed away from the beaten path into weird and wonderful places. Because who you are is more than a 'placement'.

THE HUNGER GAME

Aruj Garg
(National Law School, Bangalore)
BHUKKAD

As a third-year student at National Law School, Bangalore, Aruj Garg started a takeaway food joint to cater to the many *bhukkads* on campus. He now plans to take the Bhukkad brand of 'natural fast food' to people everywhere.

Anyone who aspires to study law dreams of getting into the National Law School (NLS). Aruj Garg was one among thousands of such Class 12 students. And he was lucky enough to actually make it.

NLS is a fantastic campus to be in – Aruj simply loved it. What he didn't like, however, was 'law' itself. So he started looking around, seeking inspiration in books and people around him.

"I heard of a senior – Ankur Singla – who'd started a company called akosha.com. So I mailed him and said I'd like to do an internship."

Aruj quickly understood the crux of entrepreneurship: it's all about solving a problem. The biggest problem he could see on campus was 'food'.

The solution – a student-friendly takeaway food joint by the very apt name of 'Bhukkad'.

The college authorities were hesitant. Why should a law student go into business? But beyond the laws created by humans, there is the law of nature.

Each one of us is blessed with *some* special talent.

Each one of us is meant to contribute *something* to this world.

As the snake sheds its skin by rubbing itself against a rock, college is that process where you have a chance to shed your inhibitions. Try something unusual.

Find your true calling in life.

THE HUNGER GAME

Aruj Garg
(National Law School, Bangalore)
BHUKKAD

Aruj was born and brought up in Chandigarh.

"I studied at Hansraj Public School, Panchkula, where I was the headboy and very active in extracurriculars, especially debating and public speaking."

In fact, he was rarely in the classroom, yet also a good student. Since his father was a lawyer, Aruj was inclined towards law at an early age. And his dream was to enter the top-ranked National Law School (NLSIU, Bangalore). After months of rigorous preparation, Aruj cracked the CLAT (Common Law Admission Test) and got through.

"The first couple of years were amazing. There was so much to learn and it felt great to be in the best law school in the country."

But slowly and steadily, Aruj realised he did not enjoy law – as a subject. He could not imagine spending the rest of his life in the legal profession – it was not his calling. By the third year of college, Aruj was busy reading books like *Stay Hungry Stay Foolish* and *Connect the Dots* in the classroom.

"I was also fascinated by Captain Gopinath's biography, *Simply Fly*. These books introduced me to the idea of entrepreneurship."

Aruj had heard of a senior from the batch of 2007 who had started his own company. The senior was Ankur Singla and the startup was Akosha - an online forum to resolve consumer complaints. Aruj took up a one-month internship with the company in February 2011.

"At that time, we had one computer, one desk and there was no other employee!"

Working with Akosha was an eye-opening experience. Every day there were small challenges to overcome, and small victories to celebrate.

"I still remember, one day, we got 4 clients and we were overjoyed - that was such a big deal!"

After hours of discussion with Ankur, Aruj realised that the thing an entrepreneur really needs is a problem - a 'pain point' - to solve. And what bigger point for hostelers than food? No matter which campus you go to, nobody is happy with the mess *ka khaana*.

"So, I thought, why not we start a small food joint on campus? A couple of my friends also said it was a good idea, let's do it together."

The plan was to pool in ₹20,000 each, as initial capital. But at the discussion stage itself, both the friends backed out. There was pressure from parents, worry that it might affect their studies.

"Even my parents had put this condition - 'You cannot fail in any of your subjects. You have to maintain the same CGPA.'"

Aruj assured them, "I won't let you down, I promise!"

One thing Aruj was clear about - he wouldn't ask his parents for money. Putting together some funds was, therefore, the first challenge. By saving most of his internship stipend and working on a research project at NLS, Aruj finally got ₹25,000 in hand.

"I remember, there was this Facebook contest where I got all my friends to like a page. So, you know, there are all kinds of ways to make some cash!"

Ankur Singla of Akosha also put ₹10,000 into the venture, simply because he liked the concept.

Now came the time to get permission from the authorities. And that took a good bit of convincing. Initially, there were apprehensions about maintaining hygiene and quality. The more fundamental question was – should a law student be encouraged to start a business?

"They were hesitant but I was persistent and, eventually, they agreed."

The President of the Student Association, Ajar Rab, was very supportive and so was the vice-chancellor, Professor Venkata Rao. The college permitted Aruj to occupy a small empty space – about 100 sq feet – for a nominal rent of ₹1000 per month.

The question now was – what to sell?

"Initially, I thought of buying food from outside and selling it. But I realised that won't work out."

To develop his own menu, Aruj converted his own hostel room into an experimental 'kitchen'. With a few utensils and a *sasta* hotplate, the cooking and tasting began. In the cooking part, he was ably assisted by Shwetank Ginodia, a batchmate who had a good sense of 'what will taste good'.

"We used to literally give out free food to people in the hostel and ask, 'How do you like it?'"

Friends would drop in at night to meet, eat and brainstorm – how to make the hotdog better? What kind of sauces to

"If it was an MBA campus, it might have been different. For a law campus it was difficult for people to accept the fact that I was doing something which was totally unrelated to law."

"College authorities may say 'no' initially. But if you persist with it, keep going back again and again, they will say yes."

use? The trial and error method yielded a lot of disasters but also a few 'hits' like the chicken salami sandwich.

One thing Aruj was very clear about – as little cooking as possible.

"We wanted to be an assembly unit, like Subway. They were my big inspiration."

The Subway model is to put everything together when the customer wants it – fresh, healthy and quick. The final piece of the puzzle was a name for the venture. 'Bhukkad' was suggested by an NLS junior, Vikram Shah, and Aruj knew in an instant – *this* is it.

The Bhukkad takeaway opened for business on 1 May 2011 with a menu of pizzas, sandwiches and burgers. There was a lot of excitement on campus and the first day's sale was ₹5300.

"Initially, there was a novelty factor, people tried different things. After a month, we settled into constant sale of ₹2000-3000 per day."

The Bhukkad Café opened when classes got over at 1:30 pm and shut at 10 pm. Initially, Aruj was there himself, managing the cash counter as well as dispensing the food. Friends would often drop by and help, some would just hang around and play music.

"It became a community place where everybody would come, chill and have a good time. And that's what I always wanted it to be."

But you cannot run a business day after day with volunteers, you need staff. Eventually, Aruj persuaded the night watchman on campus to join him. Apart from a better salary, the big incentive for him was 'no night duty'.

There is no rocket science involved in this business – there is a Standard Operating Procedure (SOP). 'Training' means standing there with your employee, explaining what needs to be done until he gets the hang of it.

"I also used to write down the SOP and give it to them in their own language."

Things were going smoothly but then came HR issues. One employee suddenly decided to quit, while another came in and left even before work started. At this point, Aruj had no option but to shut down Bhukkad for a period of 6 months (January–June 2013).

"I realised, I cannot be dependent on one employee and restarted it myself."

Assisted by a part-timer who came in the morning and did some basic preparation, Aruj was back in business. Even if it meant being at the counter all day, with just a two-hour break. Again, there was a lot of support from friends – people started coming in and helping.

Gradually, things stabilised and Aruj now spent only about an hour a day at the outlet. Mostly to keep tabs on the inventory and deal with any minor issues. Monthly sales were in the region of ₹30,000-35,000 with a neat profit of ₹5000-8000. That took care of eating out, movies and travel expenses.

"I was happy because I didn't have to ask my parents for pocket money!"

Meanwhile, true to his word, Aruj was maintaining his grades – he was having the best of both worlds. But, at the end of the fourth year, it was time to make a tough decision. Everybody advised him to get some 'experience'.

"The idea was never to cook something when someone ordered it. It should be precooked, refrigerated and just assembled."

"It's not about how many hours you study, it's about how smartly you do it. In that way, I was able to manage both things."

"If you don't want to work with a law firm, work at a food enterprise," they said.

A fire raged in his mind for days and weeks – what was the right thing to do?

"Eventually, I decided that I had the momentum so it was logical and sensible for me to continue."

Back on campus, there was a brief period when Aruj wavered. While he had no interest in joining hotshot corporate law firms like AZB Partners or Amarchand Mangaldas, he was fascinated by McKinsey. And he did apply for a job with the company.

"McKinsey has a two-year program after which you can do an MBA. I went for the interview but didn't get selected."

After that, it was back to Bhukkad with renewed focus and vigour. In February 2013, Aruj did a two-week stint with Faaso's which was just about to launch in Bangalore. He randomly emailed the founder of the company, asking if he could work there – not for a salary, just for the experience.

"Faaso's is also a startup, but they've got funded and grown quite big, so now they have processes and systems in place."

Working with Faaso's helped Aruj understand the nitty-gritties of the business – operations, costing and marketing. At the end of two weeks, the law student was confident that he could take his own venture to a similar scale.

After graduating in July 2013, Aruj started the process of incorporating the company and going 'professional'. A cousin based in London came forward as an angel investor and advisor.

So far, Bhukkad had been operating without a license, nor did it pay taxes. This style of working had to change.

4 separate licenses are required to run a food establishment in Bangalore and they are not easy to get. Either you sweat it out yourself or hire a consultant. The 'rate' is ₹10,000 per license, including the grease component.

"Since I didn't have that kind of money, I had to learn it the hard way. It took me 5 months to understand, but I finally got my license."

So why take all this trouble? Because when you are bigger and looking for investors, they will look for compliance. A professional setup which is registered with the government and pays its taxes also helps when it comes to attracting talent.

In October 2013, Aruj hired a professional chef, a hotel management graduate with two years of experience at a five-star hotel.

"I needed somebody to handle the operations completely, someone who understands food safety."

But how did Aruj persuade Chef Sandesh M S to leave a 5-star kitchen for a startup? While a luxury hotel seems glamorous from the outside, the pay is low and the working hours crazy.

"I knew I would have to offer more money but apart from that, I said to him, 'This is a challenge. Here, you will be in charge of the entire operation.'"

The entrepreneur is selling a dream, a vision of 'how things will be'. While the ground reality may be quite different.

The 'entire operation' was actually being run from Aruj's one-bedroom flat in Banashankari, with a Maruti Alto serving as a 'delivery van'.

"It took me 5 months to understand the ins and outs of how to get licenses. Now I know how to get work done from government officials."

"We explored all over Banglaore where to get the cheapest raw material so that we can keep our prices low."

"The immediate goal before us was to start 3 more Bhukkad outlets and prove that this model worked!"

The logical thing to do was to expand to more campus locations. But this idea ran into a practical hurdle. Most colleges are shut for 4–5 months a year – including vacation, preparatory leave, Sundays and festivals. Thus, a pure college model is not sustainable. But, take away the location and there is nothing 'unique' about Bhukkad.

"Dominos stands for pizza, McDonalds for burgers – we had a little bit of everything."

And, as a no-frills, takeaway-style outlet, Bhukkad could certainly not offer 'ambience'. So, then what? While this problem was churning in the young man's head, a different problem was churning in his stomach. The problem of 'what should I eat tonight'.

In July 2013, Aruj was diagnosed with high cholesterol – an unusual affliction at his age. This severely limited his food options. Chips, biscuits, ice cream and pretty much all processed foods became a no-no.

"My eating-out options boiled down to Subway sandwiches and idlis!"

With discipline and common sense, Aruj managed to bring his cholesterol down but he was struck by one thought. Why can't fast food be healthy? And taste good at the same time? This thought provoked a lot of research and Aruj found enterprises in the UK and USA* which serve 'natural' fast food, i.e. food prepared using minimal preservatives and processed elements.

---

* Chains like Paninaro and Crostini follow the 'natural fast food' philosophy.

"The menu has options which contain fat, but it is 'good fat'. That's the kind of food I like!"

Thus Bhukkad 2.0 was born – older, wiser, healthier. An afforable 'quick service', natural, fast food brand, open to any sort of location and a wider audience. In particular, the large population of young executives and IT workers who rarely cook at home. Aruj discussed the concept with his angel investor and received a thumbs up.

"We are now scouting for locations in business parks and areas which have a large office crowd."

The success of this idea greatly depends on coming up with the right menu. And to that end, Chef Sandesh and LLB Aruj are creating a whole new set of 'food laws' – to cover every kind of recipe in their kitchen. The 'Bhukkad Code' stipulates 'no processed meat', 'no white bread' and 'no packaged dressings'. The idea is to take fresh ingredients and cook them in a healthy way, in the company kitchen.

"For egg-based dressings, we use only egg whites. And we've found that hummus is a great replacement for mayonnaise!"

In addition, the Bhukkad kitchen exclusively uses olive oil. Which is all very good, but what about the cost factor? This is where the experience in catering to the very price-sensitive student-market comes in handy.

"In a college market, we introduced salads at the price of a sandwich – it was a big hit. And yes, we made money on it. We had done calculations to the last paisa."

The trick is to provide healthy offerings without escalating prices. After a lot of *daud-dhoop*, Aruj has found a vendor who is ready to supply wholewheat breads at an affordable price.

"Everybody else is doing their roles and I'm the troubleshooter."

"Wholewheat will be the default option. If we ever use 'normal' white bread, it will be charged extra."

The vendor said, "Since you are a startup, I want to help you. I'll give you this bread at a cheaper rate than what I charge restaurants."

Despite all these measures, prices at the Bhukkad outlet in NLS have gone up by 15–20%. But, surprisingly, sales have *increased* by 30%. All thanks to innovations in the menu such as the 'Asian Green Salad' (beans, cauliflower and lettuce with a sweet-lime and honey dressing, and roasted peanuts sprinkled on top).

"We have customers who 'book' it in advance! Another popular item is the 'Mexican Bean Sandwich' made with in-house salsa, rajma and jalapenos."

These innovations are a result of daily experiments in the kitchen where everything must pass the filter of: 'is it natural'. This can lead to inspired alternatives. Take for example the creamy-cheesy sauce which is commonly used to cook pasta. How does one substitute something like that?

"We are trying to create white sauce with boiled cauliflower and milk!"

This idea came from NLS senior, Priyadarshini Kedlaya, who authors 'Sugarfree Sweetheart', a blog on diabetic eating.

Meanwhile at the back-end, one of the major challenges is tracking the inventory. Bhukkad has invested in a software system from a Delhi-based startup, Posist, which is on the cloud. So at any point, sitting in office, or on his smartphone, Aruj can track how much raw material is left at each outlet.

At present, there are just two full-time employees apart from the chef, but it's now time to expand. And Aruj had found an interesting way to spot the right talent. Whenever he visits a food outlet and likes an employee's attitude, he leaves behind his visiting card.

"I was at Krispy Kreme the other day and spotted this guy who simply takes orders but is a great marketer. I know I'm going to hire him 3 months down the line!"

Knowing *what* you want and *how* you're going to get it is what makes you an entrepreneur. While many wellwishers have advised Aruj to change his brand name from Bhukkad to something more 'sophisticated', he is going by his gut.

"I like the sound of Bhukkad and the name has definitely been lucky for me! But, yes, we need to work on our branding."

Once the first 3 outlets are up and running, Aruj plans to go to an outside investor who can help him go to scale.

"The goal is to set up a commerical kitchen and have Bhukkad outlets all over Bangalore. We're small right now but the dream is big."

It's an unusual dream – far removed from the practice of law. But Aruj has two of his own NLS seniors for inspiration – Sameer Singh and Matthew Chandy – who started a restaurant in London called Mooli's which became famous for its wraps (essentially rotis with fillings). They later sold it to an investor.

Aruj is just 24 – he has time and energy on his side. And he is completely focused on his idea.

"My parents have given me two years to prove this can work and I am determined to do it."

It's really about your own conviction. *Kuch toh log kahenge, logon ka kaam hai kehna*. The question is, what is the whisper of your inner voice?

Are you complacent and easily satisfied? Or do you have a bhukkad in you?

ADVICE TO YOUNG ENTREPRENEURS

Take that leap and just be at it – it will work out in some way. You might not make a lot of money initially, so be patient.

The world conspires to help you in your quest of doing something bold and big. Whenever I have needed money, I have got some paid project to do. NLS alumni have offered to help by taking care of my legal work. A design firm based in Goa did our branding work free of cost. In fact, random people have offered to help and things generally fall into place.

Just be at it. Keep doing things. Even though they won't make sense at that point. There is a larger jigsaw which is being solved in the process.

You will get a lot of support from friends. The administration will also back you once you are doing well. Initially, they might have issues, but don't stop if they say no once. They will see your passion and finally say yes.

Don't forget academics – getting your degree is important. Believe me, it's not that hard to strike a balance.

If you're still unsure, try working with startups in your vacations. That's one sure way of knowing if you are cut out for an entrepreneur's life.

FEELS LIKE HOME

Anurag Arora
(ICFAI Business School, Pune)
GANPATI FACILITIES

As an outstation student, Anurag faced accommodation issues when he joined college in Pune. He seized the opportunity to set up a hostel business for the next batch while still a second-year MBA student. In its second year, Ganpati Facilities made ₹25 lakh in profit – 5 times the salary he could have got through placement.

When Anurag Arora got an 'admit letter' from ICFAI Business School, Pune, he was on top of the world. There was just one problem - the college did not have a hostel.

So, like hundreds of outstation students, he enrolled in a privately run hostel. In good faith, Anurag paid ₹48,000 in advance - the 'fee' for the entire year. But he got a rude shock when he arrived in Pune.

"The hostel was badly maintained, badly managed... I left after just 3 days, but I lost my entire forty-eight thousand."

Man mein gussa toh tha, but what could he do? That year, Anurag stayed in a rented flat, shared with a couple of friends.

In April 2013, Anurag was in the middle of his summer internship in Delhi when he noticed a host of queries from the incoming batch on the college Facebook page. Their topmost concern was: "Where will we stay?" To complicate matters, the IBS campus had shifted to Hadapsar, a new area on the outskirts of Pune city, with no hostel providers.

Anurag *ke dimaag mein ek* idea *chamka* - why can't *I* set up my own hostel?

Hastily wrapping up his internship, Anurag arrived in Pune 15 days before the start of the new session. He located a few good flats, furnished them and signed up 75 students. That year, he juggled the second year of MBA along with running the hostel business. By the time placements rolled around, Anurag knew he didn't *want* a job.

This year the business has doubled and there is huge potential to grow further.

"My philosophy is very simple - to keep my customers happy. I, too, was a student and I know what students want."

But do you students know what *you* want? And do you have the guts to do it?

Knowing that *aaj* parents *naaraaz honge* but someday they *will* say, "*Beta*, I am so very proud of you."

FEELS LIKE HOME

Anurag Arora
(ICFAI Business School, Pune)
GANPATI FACILITIES

Anurag Arora was born in Patna.

"We are a middle class family. My dad was a government servant who always wanted me to get into IIT or IIM or become an IAS officer."

Anurag seemed to be 'on track', scoring 94.8% in Class 10. Bihar *ka mahaul us waqt kuch kharaab tha*, so he moved to Delhi for higher studies. And that's when things began going downhill.

"That's the age when people fall in love and I was in a relationship... We broke up on the verge of Class 12 boards and it affected me very badly."

While he managed to give his board exams and get a respectable score, Anurag was in so much turmoil that he could not focus on the IIT entrance. He decided to drop a year and appear with better preparation next time.

"I started my preparation and, simultaneously, joined a BPO company to earn some pocket money."

Teleperformance was an outbound BPO with very high,

unlimited incentives based on the amount of sales achieved. At the age of 18, Anurag found himself earning anywhere between ₹70,000 to ₹100,000 per month.

"That's when I lost the path. I thought, when I am earning so well, why pursue a regular course?"

Anurag enrolled himself into a BCom (Pass) with Delhi University through correspondence. Meanwhile, he was working hard and partying hard.

"I earned more than ₹30 lakh and blew it all up on clothes, movies, eating out."

Anurag also indulged his passion for cars by buying a Hyundai Sonata with the customised number plate '2222'. Life was good, but where would he go from here?

"After two years, I realised there is money but there is no future in telesales, working from 1:30 am to 9:30 am."

At this point, Anurag's father was hardly speaking to him. There was nothing to express, apart from disappointment. He had once been a teacher, whose own students had excelled and 'made it big' in life.

"So when someone used to meet him and ask, 'What is your son doing?' he used to feel ashamed."

At this point, Anurag decided to go back to studies and enrolled for the MBA entrance exam coaching with Career Launcher. Ultimately, he got into ICFAI Business School (IBS), Pune.

While everyone struggles to make it to a good college, few make good use of the time they spend there. Anurag joined IBS with a different mindset. From the very first day, he was determined to prove himself.

"I wanted to be a topper and show my dad *ki main ab bhi kar sakta hoon.*"

When the first semester results came out, Anurag had indeed topped his class. His father was finally happy. Anurag continued to perform excellently and, in April 2013, he was chosen for a summer internship by Cuponation (a sister company of Jabong). Since the project was to do with social media marketing, he spent long hours on the internet and, in particular, Facebook.

"That's when I noticed a lot of queries from newcomers on the IBS Pune FB page. Most of the queries were regarding accommodation."

Anurag was reminded of his own misadventure, when he first arrived in Pune. ICFAI Business School did not have its own hostel, hence the college had a tie-up with a private hostel. These were actually residential flats with basic furnishing, shared by up to 6 students.

"The condition of the flats was pathetic, to be frank... I was disgusted."

There was no geyser in the bathroom – you had to ask for hot water in a bucket. One Indian-style toilet was shared by all the residents. What's more, to make a little extra money, the owner had removed the granite slab in the kitchen and converted it into a 'bedroom'.

"I left after just 3 days but the fee was non-refundable, so I lost my entire forty eight thousand."

The new batch was finding it even more difficult. The college had shifted from Aundh to Hadapsar – a newly developed area of Pune. There were no private hostel vendors in Hadapsar. Yes, they could find a broker, rent a flat and share it with friends but it was all a big hassle.

"I had done that in my first year so I knew it is not easy."

All of a sudden, Anurag was hit by a big and bold idea.

"I thought, if there is no hostel provider, why don't I set one up?"

"My father was broke... emotionally broke. He thought, my son will go to IIT or IIM, *jaise har* parents *ki hoti hai* but I could not fulfil his wish."

"I can take a lower-quality flat and earn a lot more but I thought if customers are not satisfied, *aage baat nahin banegi*."

Out of curiosity, he called up the college and expressed interest in taking up this responsibility. Being the class topper, Anurag was in the good books of the management. What's more, he'd organised a couple of events on campus, so he had some kind of a track record.

And, well, the college really didn't have too many other options.

"After I got a 'yes' from the admin team of my campus, I quickly finished my summer project and arrived back in Pune."

It was the middle of May, just 15 days left for the new batch to join.

The first task was to find flats to take on rent. With the help of friends, Anurag connected with brokers and went around inspecting what was available.

"I visited almost all the residential societies near my college and spoke to owners of as many vacant flats as possible."

This was useful in doing the 'maths' of the project – certainly it looked like a good profit could be earned. But one thing Anurag was sure about – he would not compromise or cut corners in order to make a little bit extra.

"*Main khud ek* student *hoon, mujhe ek achhe* flat *mein rehne ka shauk tha toh maine socha, doosron ko bhi yehi shauk hoga*. (As a student, I wanted to stay in a nice flat and I thought, surely others will also want that facility)."

Thus, Anurag decided to take apartments in well-constructed, well-maintained buildings. These were available in plenty in the newly developed township of Hadapsar called Amanora. The rent was slightly higher and so was the deposit.

The problem was - Anurag had *no* money to invest. The college had sent his name and number to the incoming batch, so there were enquiries. But there was no 'hostel' to show.

So what Anurag did was show the students his own flat.

"It was neat and clean, well-furnished. I told them the hostel will look just like this."

One student was convinced and paid ₹54,000 as annual fees. Anurag promptly used this amount to pay the token anount for 5 good flats close to the college. He furnished one flat, showed it to prospective students and collected more fees. This money was used to pay the deposit for more flats and to buy furniture.

With business coming, it was time to create a business entity. Anurag set up a sole proprietorship and opened a bank account for the company.

"Lord Ganesha is considered to be the 'God of every home', hence I chose the name 'Ganpati Facilities'."

While a few students had signed up in advance, the majority would commit only after they arrived in Pune, along with their parents. The new batch started coming in on June 1 and Anurag barely slept the night before.

"I still remember going to the railway station at 4 am to welcome the crowd from Kolkata."

The day was a flurry of activity - talking to students, to parents, taking them for a hostel visit. Collecting cash, managing cash, completing registrations. Luckily, Anurag's mother had arrived in Pune to lend a helping hand.

"People are shocked and surprised to know I started this business from an initial investment of zero rupees."

"My mother is a homemaker but, for me, she has been a career maker. She is my biggest support."

"She briefed the parents and guardians and put them at ease. They got convinced *ki* hostel *theek hi hoga*."

What's more, Anurag made students sign an undertaking with 12 clauses – no smoking, no drinking, boys not allowed in girls' rooms and vice versa. Although it was a private hostel, it would be a hostel with rules and regulations. Anyone who broke the rules would be asked to leave and fees would not be refunded.

Out of 150 students in the batch, 75 signed up with Ganpati Facilities. Thus began a 'double life' – student by day, entrepreneur by evening and late into the night. Not an easy thing to pull off. Yet, Anurag made the best of it.

"I chose service marketing as a subject in my third semester. I learnt many valuable things that helped me take my business to the next level!"

By the time the placement process began, Anurag was clear about one thing. This business was far more lucrative than any job he could bag on campus. Hence, there was no 'dilemma'.

"The jobs I could get were paying ₹5-6 lakh p.a., while my profit in the business was more than ₹10 lakh in the first year itself."

The ICFAI Business School offers a dual degree – PGPM and MBA. In February 2014, Anurag passed his PGPM exams with flying colours. He now had 3 months to prepare for his MBA exams, as well as gear up for the new batch of students.

This time, he decided to do things differently.

"Last time, I paid ₹3 lakh to brokers to get flats. This time, I approached Kumar Builders and they put me in touch with owners directly."

Anurag was able to strike a deal with 4 such owners who were 'investors' and thus had a large number of vacant flats. By paying ₹5000 token amount, he was able to get 33 flats in the same complex. This would benefit students greatly.

"Previously, half the students were in Amanora township and half in Kumar Builders' complex. So it was difficult for me to supervise, look into any issues."

What's more, Anurag wanted 'what is best' for the students. Amanora township is swankier but means a much longer walk to the college. The Kumar complex is close to the institute, as well as an ATM, department store and a couple of good *dhabas*.

"I also made changes in my pricing after the experience of the first year."

Initially, Anurag offered two packages - one was rent only, the other included Wi-Fi and electricity for ₹500 extra per month. Not only did students become careless and run up huge bills, they expected Anurag to be on call for any internet-related issue.

"I used to get calls at midnight, saying, 'Net is down - please come and fix it'!"

The package had to be discontinued.

Anurag also changed the 'layout' of the hostel, to make it more student-friendly. In the first year, a two BHK flat housing 6 people - 2 in each bedroom, 2 in the hall. Each room had 2 beds, 2 cupboards and 2 study tables. The problem was that, invariably, one person in the room wanted to study at night, while the other wanted to sleep.

> **"My day used to start at 7 am and there was no fixed time to go back home. I still remember that I did not shave or get a haircut for two months."**

"My primary objective is to help outstation students get all the required facilities and support. I am available almost 24X7 to help them."

"There used to be fights, where I had to intervene. So I thought, let us have 3 beds in each bedroom and make the hall a common study area."

Ek chhota sa idea but one with a big impact on the quality of living.

In April 2014, the ICFAI Business School sent out the admission letter to its next batch. Along with details of the hostel options. This time, Ganpati Facilities was not the only vendor – there was competition. But Anurag remained confident.

"My primary objective was to help all the outstation students to get a 'home away from home' with all the facilities."

To convey this, Anurag prepared a 'prospectus' which included photographs and testimonials from students – both girls and boys. While 50-60 students signed up on the basis of the prospectus, paying the fee online or via DD, the majority wanted to 'see and buy'.

The month of May was spent furnishing the 33 flats – a giant exercise where more than 150 beds, mattresses and cupboards had to be physically shifted.

"I used to do the shifting late at night so that I don't cause disturbance to the neighbours."

Each flat also comes with common amenities like curtains, geysers, dustbins, doormats, a fridge and a washing machine. This is unusual for a private hostel and thus an added attraction.

"At present, I don't provide food but I have tied up with

dabbawalas to give tiffin at reduced prices. Same with presswalas and maids."

Instead of pocketing the commission, Anurag simply passes on the benefit of 'bulk discount' to his students. At the end of the day, it's about winning the trust of your customer and here, Anurag's experience comes handy.

"I have to sell my seats, the other vendor is also selling his seats. So how I communicate, parents *se main kaise baat karta hoon,* makes a big difference."

When Anurag meets parents from Patna, he handles them in 'Patnawala style'. When he talks to parents from Delhi, he becomes a Dilliwala. But most importantly, he does not exaggerate or make false claims.

"One thing I learnt in telesales is that you have to be very careful what words you use. Always better to under-promise and over-deliver!"

This he does by being a friend, mentor and guide to his students. At 5 pm, 'Anurag *bhaiyya'* is on the hostel premises, available to anyone who needs help with their studies. Or advice regarding their career.

"My father always said *ki* knowledge *baatne se badhati hai.* So I am happy to share my knowledge!"

As a result, several students managed an 'A' grade in their recent college exams.

Another area Anurag looks into is recreation. He has taken the hostellers on 4-day trips to picnic spots near Pune - all at his own expense. But why take all this trouble? Because it keeps the students - and the neighbours - happy.

"I have to keep the building society people happy, so I try to avoid parties from taking place in hostel campus. At the same time, students need to have some fun."

Apart from weekends, birthday celebrations can be a nuisance to other residents. So Anurag maintains a list of birthdays and makes sure he is there until the cake is cut at midnight.

"Somehow, I have to maintain that balance," he smiles.

"I should thank that uncle who did not refund my ₹48,000 hostel fee. *Uska mujhe gussa tha* and see how far it took me!"

Out of a batch of 240 students, 150 have joined Ganpati Facilities. 50 are with the competition, while the rest are renting flats independently. With an annual fee ranging from ₹50–54,000 per year and 30 hostel units, Anurag's company has clocked revenues of ₹75 lakh in Year 2. And it is making a handsome profit.

The mathematics is quite simple. As a 6-seater hostel, the fee received per flat is ₹25,000 per month (₹4150X6). While the rental per month is approximately ₹15,000. Deducting the amount invested on furniture and incidentals, the net profit is over ₹25 lakh.

When you earn such a sum in a short span, the temptation is *ki dabaa lo*. Declare less income, save on paying tax, 'enjoy what you have earned'. But Anurag thinks differently. Apart from one indulgence - buying a Ford Ecosport - the focus is completely on the business.

"I want to grow my company and, to do that, to raise investment - or even take a home loan - I need to maintain proper accounts."

Thus, he makes it a point to return the deposit of ₹8000 per student at the time of leaving the hostel. A practice that many vendors do not follow, knowing they can 'get away with it'.

"I know if my students are satisfied, they will recommend my hostel to the junior batch. They are my 'brand ambassadors'."

Anurag is planning to approach other colleges in Pune to provide hostel facilities. He is also thinking of entering the corporate segment. This could be in the form of a guesthouse or providing shared accommodation to working women.

"The concept would be different – only two girls per room, with a couch in the living room and LCD TV."

Apart from accommodation, the young entrepreneur plans to start providing food facility. For this, he is enlisting the help of his mother, who has experience in corporate catering.

On the personal front, Anurag got engaged to his batchmate, Aastha Purohit, in October 2014.

"At present, she is working with Citibank and will not be joining my business."

To expand across Pune – and to other cities – Anurag will need to build a team. He will need to have systems. He will need to do a hundred big and small things.

A thousand doubts, a million decisions. But in that moment before you fall asleep, you *know*. Your life is what you make of it.

ADVICE TO YOUNG ENTREPRENEURS

I did not plan to take this path of entrepreneurship but when opportunity knocked, I seized it. My story shows that I wasn't 'born with it'. I developed an entrepreneurial bent of mind at the age of 23.

There was no venture capitalist by my side to offer me funds. Luckily, I entered an industry where the customer is willing to pay in advance.

You have to think of creative ways and means to fund your idea.

The thing is, entrepreneurship is not one of many options for me, it is the only one now. What I love about it is – independence. I decided to quit sitting for campus placements because I didn't see the point of working for someone else for the rest of my life.

Think of doing something with a good heart and an intention to help people and success will come to you along the way.

TO CATCH A THIEF

Apurva Joshi (CA Final student)
FRAUDEXPRESS

During her articleship, Apurva entered the unusual domain of forensic accounting. After working on dozens of cases, at the age of 24, she has launched a university-recognised course in the field of fraud-risk assessment.

If you are a bright student but not inclined toward engineering or medical, the natural choice is 'CA'. A safe, predictable and respectable career path.

You work hard, you pass exams, you aim for a rank. In between all this, you do an articleship at a firm owned by your uncle.

Apurva Joshi did not have any 'uncle' to fall back on. So the small-town girl came to Pune, looking for a break with a CA firm. She got that break with Indiaforensic, a small startup.

This firm was in the business of 'forensic accounting' - an unusual domain which Apurva had never heard of.

The young trainee soon found herself conducting 'fraud-risk assessment' and studying company balance sheets for 'early warning signs of fraud'.

"When the whole world was busy filing tax returns and making entries in Tally, I was doing something really out of the box!"

Some thought it was risky, they advised her to stick to taxation and audit. *Kyun aise jhamele mein padne ka?*

But Apurva was completely hooked. She spent her days and nights learning as much as possible. She enrolled for the Certified Fraud Examiner course by ACFE, USA. And then the entrepreneur within asked - "Why is there no such course designed for India?"

"I suppose, better than asking questions, one has to give the answer!"

At the age of 24, Apurva launched a diploma in 'fraud-risk assessment' on her website, with recognition by Solapur University.

Just another milestone in the journey of a young, ambitious girl. A girl who believed in herself and in her ability to clean up the world - one fraud at a time.

TO CATCH A THIEF

Apurva Joshi (CA Final student)
FRAUDEXPRESS

Apurva Joshi was born in Solapur, a small town of Maharashtra.

"My whole family background is medical. Dad – MD medicine, mother – MD gynaec, sister – MDS. But my mom told me – 'do something different'."

Hence, despite scoring 89% in her Class 10 examination, Apurva opted out of medical. She took up commerce, with the goal of becoming a chartered accountant.

After completing Class 12 in semi-English medium at Gyanprabodhini Vidyalaya, Solapur, Apurva arrived in Pune in search of an articleship. Not knowing any CA firm, she scoured the Moneycontrol website, where chartered accountants were often quoted in the context of share-market trends.

"I thought those CAs may be having a vacancy and I can try my luck for a job."

One such CA was Mayur Joshi – a 'forensic accountant'. That was intriguing and, moreover, he was based in Pune. Apurva googled the address and landed up at his office, Indiaforensic, in Navi Peth. It was her first interview with a CA firm.

Mayur said, "Articleship *mein* normally *bachche* income-tax return *bharna seekhte hain,* auditing *seekhte hain* - would you like to learn something different?"

He explained what is 'forensic accounting' and it sounded mighty adventurous.

"That time I was 18 years old. I thought - why not, this will be exciting!"

What's more, Indiaforensic was a startup so, even as an article trainee, Apurva was immediately put on the job. The task was 'fraud-risk assessment' of a big retail chain. Apurva was shocked. The word 'fraud' conjured up the image of something *khatarnaak* and criminal. She felt ill-prepared to handle it.

"All my friends said, this is too risky for a girl to get into. I was thrilled but confused. Finally, I called up my mom."

Apurva's mother said, "No work is 'good' or 'bad', *pratyek goshtitun aplyala kahi tari nawin shikayla milat asata* (every task you do teaches you something new)."

She told Apurva to apologise to 'Sir' and accept the assignment. And thus began an 18-year-old article trainee's journey into the unusual world of forensic accounting.

In March 2008, Apurva travelled to Bangalore with the Indiaforensic team. For 8 days, they scanned the retailer's accounts and ran analytic tools on their servers. Everything seemed to be in order. There was only one thing left to do - a physical inspection of the inventory. But when they approached the store manager, he was evasive.

The man said, "TVs are stacked one on top of the other - how will you open the boxes?"

Was he just being difficult, or was he hiding something? Apurva decided it was time to be a little daring.

"*Main chad gayi seedi par aur upar ke maaley par baith gayi.* (I climbed up the ladder and sat on the mezannine floor)."

She opened the first box. Empty. Second box. Empty. Third box. Empty.

"TV *ek bhi nahin tha, sirf* cardboard!"

A cardinal principle of forensic accounting – validate the data given to you. Data is not 'truth'.

While climbing down, Apurva accidentally broke a box of detergent powder. She was worried – what to do now? Should they offer to pay for it?

"We decided to keep quiet and see what procedure the store follows."

The box was taken to the auction room and sold to one of the employees at 50% discount.

"We realised this could be another modus operandi for fraud!"

This first assignment was an eye-opener. Fraud was not something committed only by politicians. Ordinary people like you and me could also be cheating their employers. A salesman might give false bills for petrol. A purchase manager could leak information to a rival. A CFO may siphon money into his personal account.

"I realised that fraud is like God – it is everywhere!"

We cannot pinpoint the presence of God but we can pinpoint the presence of fraud. One way to do this is to scan a company's balance sheet. As, apart from employee fraud, the second – and bigger – kind of fraud is by the management itself. Figures are manipulated in order to show better quarterly results and push up the price of their stock.

To check this, the ICAI (Institute of Chartered Accountants) was conducting a study titled 'Early Warning Signals of Corporate Fraud', in partnership with Indiaforensic.

"All my friends told me this field is too risky for a girl to get into... But I never felt so."

"When the whole world was busy filing tax returns and making entry into Tally, I was doing something really out of the box."

"The purpose of the project was to set the benchmark – that, what are the 'red warning' signals in a balance sheet which indicate *kuch* problem *hai*."

Fate had thrown up a fantastic opportunity for a young trainee. Apurva worked tirelessly on this prestigious project. What were the accounting practices used by errant companies? Fraud *karne ke tareeke kya kya hain*?

"To find out this information, we surveyed more than 300 CAs and examined the balance sheet of 6000 companies listed on the Bombay Stock Exchange and National Stock Exchange."

The results of the study were startling. More than 1200 listed companies were indulging in some form of financial fraud*. The findings made headlines in national newspapers, including the *Economic Times* and *Mint*. In one of the news reports, Apurva Pradeep Joshi was quoted as the 'Chief Research Officer' of Indiaforensic.

"It was the proudest moment of my life because my name, along with my father's name, was quoted in newspapers!"

However, Apurva learnt a hard lesson – when you do something 'good', a few will appreciate you, but many more will criticise you.

"We started getting calls from government officials, regulators. At the same time, there were many who doubted our findings."

The report was published in September 2008. 4 months later, the Satyam scam broke and suddenly 'forensic

* Methods include inflating expenses, deferring revenues or avoiding taxes.

accounting' was hot. There were endless enquiries from the media, invitations to speak on television. Apurva's boss, Mayur Joshi, was invited by the CBI to advise the multi-disciplinary investigation team scanning Satyam.

"That was the day I found my idol. I decided that I want to be something like my boss!"

But what was the path her career should take? Was there a future in working with a small firm, in a very new field? Or was it wiser to aim for one of the 'Big Four'* accounting firms?

"I went to my native town to talk to my mother. I used to consult Ma on almost everything."

When Apurva narrated the nature of her work, Ma was astonished. Accounting *mein aisa sab bhi hota hai?* Though a doctor by profession, she sensed the potential in this atypical field. But, unlike taxation or audit, forensic accounting would not be a 'desk job'. There would be no regularity, no 'routine'.

"Ma gave me her blessings. She said, 'Go anywhere, do what you wish – pursue your dream'!"

Apurva decided that CA or no CA, she would acquire all the knowledge available in her field. She enrolled for various online certifications, including CFAP (Certified Forensic Accounting Professional), CBFA (Certified Banking Forensic Accountant) and CAME (Certified Anti-money Laundering Expert).

"I took up these courses to prepare my base since my ultimate goal was to appear for the CFE (Certified Fraud Examiner) exam offered by ACFE, USA."

At the same time, she decided to master the technical side of the profession – both the software and hardware tools. One such tool is EnCase – a small device which looks like a pen drive but is much more potent. Once inserted into a laptop, it can take a 'ditto image' of that hard drive. In fact,

* Ernst & Young, PricewaterhouseCoopers, Deloitte and KPMG are known as the 'Big Four' accounting firms.

"Many CAs indulge in unethical practices these days. Our work is exactly opposite of that."

when you run the program, it will even retrieve the deleted data and email history.

"It was a difficult tool to learn but *maine seekh liya*. I was told *ki* you are the first lady to master this tool in the country."

The issue with ICAI faded away and Apurva continued with her articleship. But continued to toil for her other courses. In October 2010, Apurva became one of the youngest Certified Fraud Examiners in India. She was just 20 years old.

No doubt Apurva was a diligent student, but what really helped her clear 4 tough papers with more than 75% marks, was her practical exposure.

"We used to get a lot of cases of big companies and, being a small firm, I got a chance to work on many of them."

These assignments came through regulatory bodies and large banks wanting 'due diligence' on companies seeking loans. As well as training for their AGMs and DGMs on how to read a balance sheet, how to detect fraud.

"Every case is a challenge but over time you can see the pattern.".

The toughest nuts to crack were the ones referred to Indiaforensic by the Economic Offences Wing (EOW) of the Maharashtra state police.

One such case was a ponzi scheme* called 'Global Travel'**. This scheme promised super-normal returns, claiming to use your money to purchase vehicles. These cars would be

* A fraudulent scheme where investors are promised high returns but money is paid out by collecting money from more investors.

** Name changed due to a confidentiality clause.

rented out as taxis and the rental money was to be given as a 'return'. The mastermind was Hafiz Aziz*, a gentleman whose spit and polish fooled thousands of small investors.

"Aziz was also laundering the black money of a well-known politician."

After collecting crores of rupees, one fine morning, Hafiz Aziz disappeared. However, the politician he had duped made a hue and cry and the man was tracked down and arrested. The problem was, Aziz was refusing to talk. At this point, the police requested Indiaforensic for help.

"Since it was a case of financial fraud, they needed to know what was the modus operandi, where are the bank accounts, how much money can be recovered."

For 4 days, the same drama continued. Aziz would sit on a bench, staring back at his interrogators. Not answering a single question. His only response would be to look here and there and keep smoking a cigarette. And that gave the interrogation team an idea.

"Let's take away the smoke from the chain smoker."

The following day, the jail staff was given strict instructions not to provide Aziz with a cigarette under any circumstances. And no water as well. By that evening, Aziz was fidgety and restless. He broke his silence and explained in detail *kya kiya, kaise kiya*.

"You never felt scared?" I ask Apurva.

"*Nahin. Kabhi nahin*," she replied, without hesitation.

Any threats?

"Just one time. We were investigating a very big travel fraud by an employee. Every day we used to get one blank call.

"It was a bit disturbing but, by the fifth day, I noticed a peculiar thing. The call always came when we were in the hotel lobby.

"We noticed one guy sitting with a newspaper covering his

---

* Name changed due to a confidentiality clause.

"I spent many sleepless nights researching various frauds in India."

face. It was the same fellow. We informed the client and they took the necessary action."

3 years quickly whizzed by and, by mid-2011, Apurva had completed her articleship. She would soon appear for the CA Final exam. The future was bright – she could continue working with Indiaforensic and advance her career. But, Apurva had other plans.

"I decided to start my own venture in order to see my potential – to walk on a new path without the *chhatrachhaya* of Mayur Sir."

Apurva had made up her mind to do something big and bold. Something that would make her famous.

"I had read *Stay Hungry Stay Foolish* and *Connect the Dots* and it inspired me to write something similar."

Apurva decided to focus on women in the domain of forensic accounting. She interviewed several such professionals who had very interesting stories. But would a book on such a niche domain appeal to the general public?

"I thought it would be better to set up a news portal about fraud. At that time, I knew 3 top names – 'Express', 'Times' and 'Today'."

The domain name 'fraudexpress' was available – Apurva quickly registered it. She was now on her own – without the support of a firm. Without colleagues. Without any brand name.

"After leaving Indiaforensic, I realised it is not easy to get an assignment!"

Even as a junior employee, Apurva had won the trust of her clients. It would have been easy to approach them and ask for business. But Apurva willingly chose the harder path. She got in touch with companies organising conferences in the field of audit and accounting and offered to cover their event on her website.

In this manner, Apurva got the chance to attend a CII-KPMG conference in Delhi and meet some high-profile corporate professionals. She eagerly collected their business cards and chatted up strangers during the coffee breaks.

"So, young lady – what can you do for us?" boomed one senior professional.

"Everything – from training to digital forensic investigations," replied Apurva.

"Really? And who will do all this?" he asked.

"I will do it," said Apurva.

The gentleman was not convinced. And he shared the reason for it. The quantum of work was huge – it could not be handled by a single person. He gave one sound piece of advice to the young entrepreneur.

"You need to build a team."

This was a very valid point. After all, even at Indiaforensic, there was a core team. Like in 'CID', each player had his own role.

"I always thought of Mayur as 'ACP Pradyumna', Sarang as 'Daya' and our Abhijeet as 'CID Abhijeet'. We also had Venkatesan Sir as 'Dr Salunkhe'!"

The task before Apurva was to build an equally competent team. But though she knew some good people, there was no money to pay them. Hence, it was more on the basis of 'trust'.

Apurva's former roommate, Manci Inamdar, was the first to join her. Manci was very good at finance and the first thing she did was to make a business plan for the digital media venture. This plan was presented to a group of investors called 'Mumbai Angels'.

"It was appreciated but, being in a niche market, we did not receive any funding."

In December 2011, Apurva decided to shift her base to Solapur for personal reasons.

"As a forensic accountant, you have to think beyond what is in front of you."

"It was a call from within, that my mother needs me, I should be somewhere close to her. I can continue working from anywhere."

In fact, Apurva was able to negotiate an assignment from a biotech company in Solapur itself. The case required computer forensics, as well as financial forensics. Apurva built a 'project team' by enlisting the aid of another agency, as well as her ex-colleague, Sarang Khatavkar. The assignment was a great success and resulted in a handsome paycheque.

"I was excited and looking forward to a bright future."

But a dark cloud was on the horizon. Soon after shifting to Solapur, Apurva learnt that her mother was having liver problems. By April 2012, her condition worsened and an operation became necessary.

"The operation was not a complicated one but Ma had a severe reaction to one of the drugs. Her heart stopped but luckily Papa was by her side."

Mrs Joshi was revived after a cardiac massage of almost 45 minutes. It was a miraculous recovery but 8 days later she went into a coma. She died, with her husband, children and extended family helplessly looking on.

"I was just 22 when I lost Ma... She was my best friend, my mentor, smile of my life."

In fact, Apurva was appearing for the third paper of her CA Final when this happened. She was unable to complete the rest of the exams. But, quickly, Apurva pulled herself together. *Kaam to aage badhana hi tha.*

"I wanted to do something for my mother as she was my inspiration."

Ever since completing her CFE (Certified Fraud Examiner) certification, Apurva had a strong desire to spread awareness about this little-known field. To this end, she had been working on a 'Student's Handbook of Forensic Accounting', which was almost complete. In June 2012, Apurva published the book on amazon.com, dedicating it to her mother.

"Our cash flows started and I was invited to speak to the local media in Solapur. Soon we added more books under the Fraudexpress banner."

All these books had India-specific material, which was not readily available. Well, if an India-specific book could have a market, why not an India-specific course? There are many students who cannot do a CA or CS exam, who become directionless. Neither can they afford to spend thousands on study material from USA.

"I thought – there is no university-recognised course in fraud-risk management. Why?"

In September 2012, Apurva's Indiaforensic colleague, Sarang, was visiting Solapur. She proposed the idea to him. In fact, Indiaforensic was already offering some online certificate courses, but the principals were too busy with consulting assignments to give much attention to training and content development.

"Mayur Sir agreed to work with me to design an in-depth course, similar to the CFE course I had done from USA."

The ACFE module consisted of 3000-4000 pages of study material, based on US laws. The basic structure was retained but Apurva adapted the course to suit the Indian context.

"We analysed various cases in India, their modus operandi, *kaise* solve *hua*. And we wrote down these examples one by one, literally *apne haath se*."

The course was to be in the form of distance learning – just like ACFE – with a CD-based examination.

By November 2012, the comprehensive study material was ready. The examination software was under preparation. But now came the most difficult part – convincing the university to give accreditation.

"I never thought of poaching clients of my previous firm. I wanted to build something of my own."

"*Pehle toh* university *ne mujhe* entertain *hi nahin kiya.* Then I decided to directly contact the vice-chancellor."

Apurva made it a point to arrive early in the morning and sit outside the VC's cabin. She would sit there, patiently, all day. Naturally, the VC wondered – who is this young lady?

One day, he told his secretary, 'Send her to meet me.'

"I grabbed this chance and gave him the demo on my laptop. I also explained there is a very big scope in this field."

With barely 6000 forensic accountants practicing in India, a certification would vastly improve the career prospects of MCom graduates. Since it was a distance-learning module, it could even be completed by those already working in jobs.

"I further convinced by mentioning that Solapur University would be the first to launch such a course in the country."

This would help the university improve its standing at the time of NAAC assessment.

The university asked Apurva to submit a proposal. The course content would further have to be critically reviewed by the 'Board of Studies' to ensure it was different from existing courses such as CA, CS, MCom and MBA.

"I would like to thank my colleague, Rajendra, and my mama, Dr Balkrishna Bhave, for their tremendous support in all aspects of university work."

While all this was happening, Apurva was also dealing with personal issues. After Ma's death, her father remained disturbed. Hence, Apurva could not shift back to Pune.

"For one year, I used to do up-down from Solapur to Pune every week. My ex-colleagues gave me all the support and I continued my work in this way."

While chatting with Sarang, Apurva became aware of another opportunity. Indiaforensic was so busy with investigations, there was no one available to document the investigation experiences. This was 'gold', ready to be mined.

"Sarang gave me the inside information and also suggested me that, 'If you give any proposal, I will support it in the board meeting'."

Apurva asked her friend, Manci, to make a business plan for Fraudexpress to pitch to the board of Riskpro (parent company of Indiaforensic). Her projections indicated that by developing content, Indiaforensic would be able to generate 70% more revenues. Fraudexpress had existing content and the capability to create more.

"I called Mayur officially and asked for time to present my plan to him."

The two met in Pune in February 2013 and Mayur quickly saw merit in the idea.

"We shook hands and he asked me to give everything in writing."

On Sarang's advice, Apurva kept 3 conditions, apart from the valuations. Firstly, Fraudexpress would remain independent. Secondly, she would be inducted on the board of Riskpro. And, thirdly, there would be a lock-in of at least 3 years.

"There was consensus from both the sides and, finally, I got inducted on the board of Riskpro in October 2013."

That same month, the course Apurva had proposed to the vice-chancellor received recognition from Solapur University.

"I was happy that I could contribute something for the students of my hometown and offer an affordable* course through the university."

Apurva also shifted back to Pune and threw herself headlong into work.

---

* The cost of the diploma in forensic accounting is Rs 12,000.

"After Ma died, only cases was the part I could engage in and *sab kuch bhula sakti hoon*."

One very interesting project she took up involved mapping the holdings and investments of politicians and their families in corporate India.

As politicians cannot invest money directly, they use middlemen and 'frontmen'.

"We proposed to create a database of Politically Exposed Parties (PEP)... *ki* politicians *ke kitne paise ghoom rahe hain aur kis* company *mein lage hue hain*."

This database – the first of its kind in the country – can be accessed by investors for a fee.

The year 2014 was an eventful one with more courses, more content and more services offered. Some of these include Auditor Due Diligence, Promoter Due Diligence and Vendor Due Diligence. It's most often a case of work, work and only work.

"I have to be flexible – if the client says, 'Come to Bangalore tomorrow', I will go, I never say no."

Work means no Sundays, no holidays, no friends *ke saath* timepass, no outings.

"Mayur Sir *ki* first condition *thi ki* if you want to excel in forensic accounting, you will have to sacrifice everything else."

In fact, if you search for Apurva online, you will not even find her photograph on Facebook.

"The people whom we investigate sometimes even go to jail. So I need to take such precautions."

Yehi nahin, Apurva is often so lost in her cases that there is no time even for a quick lunch. The use of a tool such as Forensic Duplicator requires unwavering attention.

"It's not that I can launch the tool and then come back two hours later!"

Sounds like an exciting but stressful life – how does Apurva cope with it? While many factors are not in her control, she has made one important rule for herself.

"I make it a point to go to the gym. *Wahan mera* stress *poora* burn *ho jaata hai.*"

Apurva also finds solace in spirituality, leaning on works such as *Charitra* by Gajanan Maharaj and *Shankar Geeta* by Shankar Maharaj (avatars of Guru Dattatray).

"These *pothis* give me mental peace at times when I feel hopeless."

Apurva's future plan is ambitious. In 5 years' time, she plans to have her own institute in forensic accounting. And ultimately go for an IPO.

"I will have a big company, with many people working under me. And I want to have a global name."

One unfinished project is the completion of her CA course. It is still a goal, though not a priority.

"Even if I don't get the CA tag, I am confident of making a mark in my field."

On the personal front, Apurva says she will consider getting married in two years' time, when she turns 27. Although she is unsure how she will manage her commitment to both work and family. At times of doubt, she takes inspiration from her mother's life.

"Ma ne kaam bhi sambhala, ghar bhi sambhala. (Ma managed both work front and home front)."

And she held her own in a corporation hospital which is completely male-dominated. A trait she seems to have passed on to her daughter.

Even after 6 years of experience, Apurva often meets clients who size up her petite frame, her youthful face and exclaim, *"Yeh? Yeh ladki kya kar sakti hai?* (What can this girl do?)"

Kya nahin kar sakti hai? There is no job too bold, too big, too tough, too tricky – if a girl really wants to do it, she can. And she will.

ADVICE TO YOUNG ENTREPRENEURS

Don't run behind degrees. If you clear your CA in the first attempt after doing a 'dummy' articleship, what is its market value? Zero. So go after practical knowledge. That is far more important.

When challenges come, you have to accept them. Do not go to your senior and say, "Show me the set practice or checklist – I will just follow that." Go, explore and find out for yourself how to do the work. These days, students don't want to experiment, they want everything on a table, in front of them. By doing that, you place limits on yourself.

Aur thoda daring *dikhana padta hai.* Be daring, be bold! Do not be afraid of anyone or anything!!

Eshwar Vikas

Sudeep Sabat

HOLY RAVA MASALA

Eshwar Vikas & Sudeep Sabat
(SRM Engineering College, Chennai)
DOSAMATIC

Two young engineers set out to create an automatic dosa machine. 3 years later, they have succeeded in producing the world's first tabletop 'dosa printer' and secured orders from 100 restaurant owners.

At 4 pm every day, classes end at SRM Engineering College in Chennai. Students mill about in the corridors and canteen, smiles on their faces.

Eager to enjoy the evening.

But there was this one dude called Eshwar Vikas who was different. Rushing after classes to catch a train to his place of work, some 50 km away. Work which came without a salary, without any 'job value'.

Work which had become an obsession, a compulsion, an end in itself.

"I got this idea of making an automatic dosa machine in my third year of college. And then I got so involved in it, I could not stop!"

Eshwar's enthusiasm was infectious. His roommate, Sudeep, joined him in this quest. The quest for a perfect machine-made, crispy, round dosa.

They went into the *galis* and bazaars of Chennai in search of parts. A real-life education in mechanics and industrial engineering, from the gurus of their trade.

Yet, the machine refused to work.

The boys sacrificed sleep, social activities and even their summer vacation – to solve the problem. When the first dosa cranked out of that crude contraption, Eshwar and Sudeep were on top of the world. *Bole toh,* like cracking IIT JEE All India Rank No. 1.

Two years later, their company is going strong. An improved, tabletop version of the 'Dosamatic' machine is now on sale to restaurant owners.

You spread an idea on the mental tawa. Then cook it with the heat of passion. You burn some, you screw up some, but you never stop trying.

Till one day, you 'get it'.

HOLY RAVA MASALA

Eshwar Vikas & Sudeep Sabat
(SRM Engineering College, Chennai)
DOSAMATIC

Eshwar Vikas was born in Vayalpadu, near Tirupati in Andhra Pradesh.

"My dad works for Vijaya Bank and he used to keep getting transferred. So I grew up in various villages in Karnataka – really small villages with 100-200 people."

In Class 1, Eshwar's family moved to a big city – Mysore. Finally, they shifted to Hyderabad where Eshwar completed Class 12. Around this time, he read *Stay Hungry Stay Foolish* and decided that he, too, wanted to be an entrepreneur.

"I thought, I need to have an IIM degree to start my own business but, first, I have to do graduation."

Like every other school kid in Hyderabad, Eshwar was attracted to engineering. But despite giving multiple entrance exams, he didn't crack any IIT or NIT. The one college that offered him admission was SRM in Chennai. And Eshwar decided to take it.

Soon after joining, he discovered the entrepreneurship

cell in his college, which was in partnership with NEN*. The E-Cell organised a talk by Mr Raj Shankar of Ichiban Consulting, a firm which advised SMEs. It was the first semester of the first year, but Eshwar did not hesitate to go up to the speaker and say, "Sir, I want to become an entrepreneur - can you help me?"

Raj Shankar told the young man, "Come to my office."

When Eshwar actually landed up there, the consultant explained a few home truths. Starting a website is not 'going into business'. You need to learn how to run a company, how to speak to people, how to get work done. Eshwar was intrigued.

"I would like to work for you and learn all those things!"

Thus, the first-year engineering student waited for college to end at 4 pm each day and made a 50 km trip across the city to the Ichiban office. There, he would work till around 9 pm and catch the local train back to the hostel, often reaching at midnight.

"The good thing about SRM was the full freedom - if you wanted to do something, you could do it."

Despite the hectic schedule, Eshwar was able to maintain 'decent' grades. The electrical engineering course was not all that demanding.

"I was never a topper but it was easy enough to get 70-80%."

At Ichiban, Eshwar started by helping with sales. In fact, the company ran a training program for students and his job was to 'sell' this course to people just like himself. The target was to enrol 30 people in each class. Eshwar contacted various colleges, spoke at events.

"I also used Facebook, which was very new at that time."

The young man quickly became proficient in sales, helping Ichiban Academy fill up 3 batches. The course, covering various business-related subjects, cost ₹2500 for 8

* NEN: National Entrepreneurship Network

Sundays. For his efforts, however, Eshwar earned nothing.

"I was not getting paid, not even for my transport. Actually, I did not want to get paid because I was learning so much!"

Some of these learnings he put into practice by setting up a food stall at 'Milan' - the SRM college annual festival. Since he had no money to book the stall, Eshwar got 5 friends to pool in ₹50 each and print a few b&w posters. The posters read:

"Pre-book your *vada pav* and *jaljeera* - get flat 20% off! No conditions apply!!"

Going from room to room in the college hostel, they sold 1000 *vada pav* tokens - a total of ₹8000. With money in hand, they approached the college authorities for a stall. Seeing their enthusiasm, the principal gave the stall, without taking payment.

"At the end of 3 days, we made a profit of ₹20,000!"

Eshwar continued with his sale job but he was getting restless. One day, he met an interesting person called Raja Ganesh at the Ichiban office. Raja was the owner of Amar Industries - a company engaged in construction, interior design, manufacturing and trading. It seemed like a large and exciting place.

Eshwar went up to Raja and said, "I want to work for you."

"How much do you want?" asked the owner of Amar Industries.

Eshwar said he wasn't expecting any compensation. But Raja insisted.

"I will feel bad if I don't pay you," he said. And offered to pay ₹5000 per month to cover the cost of transport and food.

"I did not get paid for my first job. The learning was much more than the payment they could have made."

"I used to sit the whole day in the gearbox shop to understand what is a gear, how does it work?"

Thus, in the fourth semester of college, Eshwar became PA to the CEO of Amar Industries. Again, the office was more than two hours away from college and Eshwar made a long journey up and down, returning at midnight. But this time, he had company.

"My friend, Sudeep, started coming to Amarsons with me. We were also roommates."

A native of Behrampur in southern Orissa, Sudeep Sabat was a Kendriya Vidyalaya product who had joined SRM to pursue electronics and electrical engineering. In the second year of college, Eshwar and Sudeep had shifted off-campus. Mainly because of the hostel food.

"We were sharing a one BHK flat and loved to cook our own food!"

Initially, Sudeep did not share Eshwar's interest in working after college hours. But that was because he had no interest in sales or office work. What Sudeep enjoyed was the company of machines and those were in plenty at Amarsons.

"I liked to observe the welding, cutting and grinding work. I loved the sounds made by machines."

Thus, Sudeep hung around the shopfloor, while Eshwar sat with 'Raja Sir' in the office. Since Amar Industries was engaged in a variety of businesses, the learning was diverse. The skill of a CEO lay in juggling multiple balls at one time – sending quotations, managing employees and keeping an eye on profits.

Eshwar made himself useful by being 'on call' at all times.

"Even when I was in class, I would get an sms that such and such mail has to be sent and I would do it right there on my phone."

Saturdays and Sundays being off, the entire days were spent at Amar Industries. And, from time to time, there were the usual projects, submissions and exams.

"The schedule was quite hectic - we were often sleepy during classes. But it was fun, somehow we managed!"

In the third year of college, Raj Shankar asked his young PA to do some research on chromium mines. An area he wanted to invest in.

The first thing Eshwar did was check online but there was little or no information. So he said to Sudeep, "Let's go to Orissa and find out for ourselves."

The next morning, the boys boarded the Coromandel Express to Bhubaneshwar - without a reservation.

"Since Sudeep belonged to Orissa, we thought it would be easy for us to communicate with people in the mining industry."

Well, that was not exactly what happened when Eshwar and Sudeep landed up at the Orissa Mining Corporation in Bhubaneshwar. When they approached an officer, claiming to be students doing a project on mining, he asked them to produce a letter from the college.

"We said our faculty will send an email but they wanted it by post, on a letterhead."

It was the same discouraging story at various other mining companies. Finally, the boys reached a chromium mine controlled by the Tata Group at Sukinda, a remote area more than a 100 km from Bhubaneshwar.

"There was no direct train or bus, but somehow we reached there."

The mining officer gave the boys a patient hearing. Looked at their college ID cards. And relented.

"Always remember, in life you have to take permission... but since you have come all the way from Chennai, I will help you."

He connected them to his technical team, who gave a

detailed presentation. In fact, they even shared a CD with the boys and wished them good luck.

"We felt bad that we were cheating them but, somewhere, we were also thrilled that we have cracked the problem of how to get the required information."

On returning to Chennai, Eshwar submitted his report. Based on which the boss went ahead with an investment. The side effect of this project was that Eshwar and Sudeep realised they could work together as a team.

"We felt it's time we start our own company!"

Around this time, the boys travelled to Delhi for some college work and, at Bikanerwala in Karol Bagh, they discovered that a masala dosa can cost ₹130. Coming from Chennai, it was a rude shock. Why was south Indian food so expensive?

The shopkeeper explained, "I have to pay ₹20,000-25,000 per month to the cook who makes dosas. So the cost goes up."

Could there be a machine that made hot, round, crisp, tasty dosas? The crazy idea came to Eshwar, he shared it with Sudeep, who heartily agreed – 'let's try it!'

Back in Chennai, the boys tried to make a 'google sketch' (a basic 3-D drawing). But that failed. So they went to a local CAD centre with a budget of ₹2000 and asked for a 'draft'. It took 3 full days, morning till night, sitting with the designer – explaining the crude idea.

"We are not from the mechanical side, so we did not even know what is a ball bearing. We just said – 'make a pillar'."

Then the designer would ask, "What size? What thickness? What material?"

Eshwar and Sudeep had no idea. But having cracked so many problems together, they were confident, *yeh bhi ho jayega*. They went to Parry's – the market for industrial items in Chennai – looking for some direction, some clue.

"80% of the shopowners won't even talk to you, they will say, tell me which part you want – 562 B or 562 C?"

But if you stuck around, waited for that free moment in his day, you would definitely learn things. You take those nuggets of information and start searching on the internet, to get more knowledge. The next morning, you go to another shop and sit there – till the owner can talk to you for a few minutes.

"Slowly, slowly, we got to know each and everything about mechanical parts."

The one thing you need to learn in this way is time. Which meant bunking quite a bit of college. Giving proxy attendance. Some of the faculty knew that these boys were doing something – they turned a blind eye.

At the end of 5 months, Eshwar and Sudeep went to another CAD designer and confidently gave their specifications. Once the design was ready, they went to Amar Industries and requested a small space in the factory.

"We had estimated, it will take a month to manufacture the machine."

Work began in January 2012 but it stretched on and on. At the end of 3 months, the boys were still nowhere near a finished product.

Making a machine from scratch is a bit of trial and a lot of error. And it costs money. The machine Eshwar and Sudeep had conceptualised was 1 metre by 1 metre – it weighed 300 kg. The cost of steel alone was Rs 80,000 (Rs 280 per kg).

"We spent ₹2 lakh from our own pocket!"

Of his ₹5000 salary per month, Eshwar used to transfer ₹4000 to his father right away. Resisting the temptation to 'enjoy it'. In this way, he had saved close to ₹1 lakh. This

"The dosa machine was a totally new concept, so we had to keep imagining and doing it. Always changing and tweaking things."

"I was not a mechanical engineer or a designer. I did not know how to run a company but I had to do this somehow... no matter what, I had to do it."

money now came in handy. Eshwar's father agreed to contribute another lakh.

The boys had two and a half months of summer vacation and decided to stay back in Chennai, to work on the machine. The toughest part was the summer heat.

"There used to be 14-hour power cuts. And water cut. And, somehow, we had to get this machine running... but it never used to work!"

By this time, Eshwar and Vikas had been shifted from Amar Industries and taken space at a factory closer home. This, too, they had convinced the owner to provide free of cost.

"We said the prototype is ready – we are just making small, small changes."

The summer went by with countless failed experiments on the huge and messy contraption. Using large amounts of dosa batter – luckily a 'cheap' raw material, available for ₹20 per kg.

One fine day, the batter went in and a dosa came out. Eshwar and Sudeep were over the moon.

"It was a little burnt, not so round but, to us, it was the 'best dosa' in the world!"

Eshwar even managed to take a video which was proudly shown to anyone and everyone. And, unlike the machine, it could be carried around. It was this video which helped the boys win the first prize in the category 'innovation' at Ventura 2012 – the business-plan competition at NIT Trichy.

Gagan Aggarwal of the Indian Angel Network liked what he saw and offered to 'incubate' the idea.

"You will need to make a private limited company and we will take a 5% stake."

In return for this, Indian Angel Network would assign a mentor who would call once or twice a month and 'guide' the boys on how to run the company.

"Some people said, 'No, 5% is too much - you are not getting any money or an office.'"

But Eshwar had a contrary view.

"I said, the idea is actually worth nothing today. If I give 5%, something will happen."

In the process, Dosamatic also got registered as a private limited company. And things got 'serious'. Till this point, the boys had thought of the dosa machine as a 'project', Now, it was a business.

When Eshwar and Sudeep returned to college for the seventh semester, the head of the department summoned them.

"Can you give a demo of your machine?"

Representatives of the US-based ABET (Accreditation Board for Engineering and Technology) were visiting SRM College of Engineering. The dosa machine was exhibited as a 'live project' and impressed the ABET team. The college got accreditation.

"The authorities asked us to submit a proposal and, within 3-4 months, we got a grant of ₹1.5 lakh."

This helped the young entrepreneurs to refine their crude prototype. They roped in a friend - Anirudh Nath - who was an electronics whiz.

"He used to do only two things in life - sleep and tinker with gadgets!"

"If a software goes wrong, you can just do backspace and 'delete', but with hardware you have to junk the piece and start all over again."

"I knew Eshwar won't feel good if his partner is sitting for placement. That means he is not confident about the company."

Various other classmates joined the bandwagon - only to quickly drop out. Entrepreneurship seemed like something big and exciting. But the hard work it entailed killed their enthusiasm.

"We were always looking for a third co-founder but never found one!"

In fact, friends became 'the enemy'. They would call and say - "There's a beachhouse party tonight." And Sudeep would say to Eshwar, "Let's go."

Eshwar would remind him, "There's work to be done."

No time for friends. No time for girlfriends. After working till 2 or 3 am on a Friday, the boys would head home. And, at 7 am, Eshwar would be shaking Sudeep awake.

"Let's sleep two more hours," Sudeep would mumble.

"We need to have a Ferrari soon - let's go!" was Eshwar's answer.

Within half an hour they would be back at the factory.

"Today, if I recall, you know, how I was motivated that day... I myself wonder! We had no factory, no office, no proper product. All we had was a dream."

A dream that 'we will make it happen'.

Placement season had started at college. To sit, or not to sit - that was the question. That's when this movie, *Dark Knight,* was released.

Eshwar recalls a scene where Batman falls into a well and keeps trying to escape using a rope. But he falls, again and again. And the rope saves him.

A prophet advises him, "You need to have the fear of death."

If you jump without a rope, you cannot afford to fail. That *one* motivation will really take you forward.

At that moment, Eshwar decided, "I will not take placement."

"My company has to work – there is no 'back-up' option."

Luckily, Eshwar's parents were supportive. But Sudeep had to take a more roundabout route.

"I told my parents, I am appearing for the written tests but I am not getting through – what to do?"

Finally, Sudeep's dad asked, "Are you really sitting for the placement?"

When he realised how serious his son was about his 'dosa-machine business', he gave his blessings. With just one condition.

"Work hard and make sure you get established very soon."

The push Eshwar and Sudeep needed came from B Hari. The founder of a company called On Track Systems in Kolkata, Hari had been assigned to mentor the young entrepreneurs. He came to Chennai to meet Eshwar and Sudeep and spent 4-5 hours just listening to their plans.

"At that time, we thought that we will open a hotel, instal our machine there and sell dosas."

With this plan in mind, they had named the company 'Mukunda Foods' (Mukunda is one of the names of Lord Krishna). On the lines of Saravana Bhavan (named after Lord Murugan) and Vasantha Bhavan (God of Spring).

"We thought, a successful restaurant in Chennai must have God's name in it!"

"I read biographies and books by Peter Drucker, Philip Kotler. I have no interest in novels!"

"The toughest part of being an entrepreneur is dealing with your own emotions."

The logic was that selling a machine would bring in a profit of ₹20,000. But making dosas would bring in continuous revenues - hence more profit.

Hari said, "You have made a machine which makes dosas. But setting up a restaurant which sells dosas is a totally different ballgame. You have to choose which business you want to be in."

Hari simply presented the two scenarios. The choice of 'what to do' was up to Eshwar and Sudeep. And they realised that their expertise lay in making the machines.

"From that day, we decided to focus and become a product company."

Thus, Hari became the 'charioteer' who led the boys through the battlefield of business. He shared his experience of running a company. And advised Eshwar and Sudeep to start thinking about building an organisation. Hiring salespeople, hiring designers.

"Think big and you will definitely grow big," was his mantra for success.

This meeting changed Eshwar and Sudeep's mindset. They stopped trying to 'do everything' and instead began searching for the right person to do each job.

This is how Eshwar and Sudeep began working with Mohammed Shah of D-cube Designs. A graduate of IIT Kanpur, Shah had deep knowledge of both mechanical engineering and production engineering. He gave them the idea of a 'tabletop machine' which works like a printer.

"We knew what we wanted our machine to do but the *how* part came from D-cube."

Mohammed had the knack for understanding each and

every functional requirement and converting it into a 'doable' format. Naturally, his services did not come cheap.

"D-cube asked us for ₹4 lakh – we said, 'We can't give you that much!'"

Mohammed said, "All right – just give me ₹1 lakh to start with and when your product is out in the market, I will ask you for the next instalment."

Once again, Eshwar asked his dad for money – he obliged without asking any questions. Sudeep also asked his family to contribute some amount.

By October 2012, the tabletop prototype 'Dosamatic' was ready. Eshwar and Sudeep decided to unveil it at a conference held by Indian Angels Network in New Delhi. Over 200 investors were expected to attend – it was a big opportunity to 'get noticed'.

The boys were given a 4-minute slot to pitch their product. The night before D-day, they tested the machine – it worked perfectly.

The next morning, Eshwar went on stage and started his presentation with a demo. At the press of a button, a crisp brown dosa was to roll out in front of the audience. He pressed once, he pressed twice... Lo and behold – only batter oozed out!

"I had to quickly take the mike and say, 'there seems to be a problem, we will fix it'."

Eshwar put on a brave face and switched to Powerpoint. Later, they discovered the machine had a short circuit.

"Of course, we were upset but what could we do?"

The people at the conference were all 'big shots'.

"First time in our life someone was introducing us to people like Mr Rajan Anandan, CEO of Google India."

Despite the very public failure, everyone they met was encouraging.

But this incident made them think and introspect. Should

we make our product better looking? Should we work to higher quality standards?

"That was the jerk which motivated us that the product should be perfect!"

Eshwar and Sudeep decided 'no more events' till they had a machine with consistent quality. The question was - how to get there?

When you ask such a question, it echoes in the universe and, one day, you hear an answer. For Dosamatic, the answer was Alistair D'Rozario.

One day, Eshwar was in the market, searching for some ball bearing. Alistair was working in the shop and asked him, "Dude, what do you need this for?"

When Alistair heard about this strange dosa-making machine, he got excited.

"I want to see it! Let's go to your factory!!"

Right there and then, he took out a creaking Pulsar and set off with Eshwar to their 'factory space' at Old Mahabalipuram Road (OMR), 50 km away. Alistair inspected the machine, then stayed back to work on it all night.

"I have solved your problem," he declared the next morning.

An engineering college dropout, Alistair was a true mechanical genius. He had a 'way' with machines.

Alistair came on board in February 2013, for a 'salary' of ₹5000 per month. By the end of March, the machine which used to make 5-6 dosas was rolling out 100 dosas. Without any breakdowns.

"We consulted IITians, we asked professors and industrial experts. The problems they could not solve were easily cracked by Alistair."

By December 2013, a strong, reliable, working machine was ready. Weighing just 50 kg, Dosamatic has containers for batter, water and oil. At the press of a button, the batter comes out, spreads into shape, oil is sprinkled and the batter is roasted. Piping hot dosa - ready in just 60 seconds!

It was time to once again go to Delhi and pitch the 'miracle machine' to investors. This time, it worked perfectly.

"We made plain dosas, butter dosas and masala dosas. This time, we got the funding."

While the initial plan was to raise ₹20 lakh, their mentor advised it would not be enough. He helped them write a more ambitious business plan.

"Hari Sir always used the phrase 'think big' – that's all. And he was the one who pushed our plan and gave confidence to the investors."

In June 2013, it was time to graduate from college. The same month, Eshwar and Sudeep got confirmation from the Indian Angel Network. Funds would be released, after completion of formalities.

The boys decided it was time to shift to Bangalore, a city friendlier to startups. And with less power cuts. Thus, Eshwar, Sudeep and Alistair found themselves in the Garden City. The problem was, they were still waiting for funds.

"We, somehow, scraped together small amounts and continued to work on the product."

Finally, in October, money came into the bank. By December, a commercially viable product was finally ready. Now it was time to go to hoteliers and convince them – use this product.

Led by Eshwar, a small sales team started cold calling all over Bangalore.

"It was easy when we were students. But nobody encourages a salesperson."

Persistence is the name of the game. In each area, hotels are divided and assigned by category. So one salesperson only takes care of outlets where a dosa costs less than ₹30. Another goes to quick service restaurants (QSRs) in malls.

"We pitch to them and invite them to our office to see the demo."

The ease of operation and the taste of the dosas are the main selling points. You no longer need an experienced cook or 'master' for ₹20,000 per month. Hence, although the machine costs ₹1.5 lakh, the 'break even' for a restaurant owner is just 6-9 months.

More than 90% of the orders, so far, are from quick service restaurants.

"We are getting orders from small towns like Rishikesh in Uttarakhand and Srikakulam in Andhra."

These customers place orders after getting a demo on Skype.

In fact, enquiries started coming in from as far as Brisbane and London. The young entrepreneurs caution these customers that, in case of a breakdown, they will have to send the machine back to India at their own cost. And they say, 'no problem'.

The first batch of machines rolled out of the factory in March 2014. While welding and cutting work is outsourced, the assembly is done completely in-house. Sudeep oversees the entire production, while Alistair is troubleshooter, designer and R&D – all in one.

"We have a tolerance level as low as 0.01 mm, hence we want to make the machine ourselves. As volumes grows, we may have to outsource."

Dosamatic estimates that, each day, Indians consume over 1 billion dosas. Imagine the potential market for a 'home' version of the current machine. The team is already working on it.

"In 5 years' time, our dream is that every house which has a microwave oven should have a dosa machine!"

In its first year-ending, 31 March 2014, Mukunda Foods had 30 confirmed orders and 15 employees (4 in sales and the rest in manufacturing). At present, the focus is not on numbers but on getting the business model right.

"We are setting up service centres with ITI diploma-holders in different cities. Our objective is to have happy customers and positive word of mouth."

In the age of Apple, it's not easy to satisfy the user.

"Someone asked if there is an inbuilt 'app' to operate the machine from a phone!"

No doubt, the goal is to keep improving. But to reach that level of sophistication may take many years. Instead of waiting to create the 'perfect' product, Eshwar and Sudeep believe 'just do it' and keep listening to customers. Strive to get better with every new batch of product.

From students to inventors to commercial entrepreneurs – it's been quite a journey for Eshwar and Sudeep. Along the way, they learned to solve problems, deal with different people, manage their money and manage themselves.

"We have seen friends who started companies and failed, all due to emotional failure."

There is also the question in every engineer's mind – 'Do I need an MBA?' Eshwar and Sudeep say, 'No'. Be it finance or marketing, you don't need to learn it in a classroom. The main challenge is managing people and that won't get any easier with a degree. It starts with finding the people who 'fit in' with your organisation.

"We don't see marks when we hire, because that's not important. We give a live project as a 'test'."

Within the company, Eshwar and Sudeep have worked out a 'good cop', 'bad cop' routine. Sudeep is always kind-hearted with employees, while Eshwar is the strict one. And this seems to work quite well.

As it's still an early phase in the company, both founders and employees work on Saturdays and even Sundays.

"Our people understand the urgency. On Sundays, they sometimes come to office with their wives and girlfriends!"

There is a long way to go. Many hurdles to cross. Many mountains to climb.

With your eyes on the road and hand on your heart, you *will* get there.

ADVICE TO YOUNG ENTREPRENEURS

Sudeep

Start when you are in college, don't think – "I will start something after I pass out." That will never happen, you will join some company, and once money starts coming into your pockets, you won't think beyond!

An idea is not enough, you need to develop a prototype. Then go out and test it in the real world. Not just in college, where everyone knows you.

If you can get incubation at IIMA CIIE, Nasscom or other such organisations, go for it. Not for the money but to get correct exposure and guidance from mentors. It will also make you focus on your revenue model, make you serious about running a business.

Lastly, many people may promise to help you but won't actually do it. So don't depend on anyone but yourself.

Eshwar

Running a startup is a marathon, running a product company is a double marathon. You need to have a LOT of patience.

Keep that passion ignited for at least 5 years. You might think, "I am very talented and will be successful faster." But it doesn't happen like that.

Don't think you are doing a 'college project'. It has to be commerical, somebody must be willing to *pay* for your product.

What we did initially was, sell dosas made from the machine. We used to sell 10 dosas, then the machine would break down, then we would fix it and start again. But we came to know our dosas are as good as what you make on the *tawa*. No one could tell the difference. That gave us the confidence – yes, this product is working. We must continue. No matter what.

START-UP RESOURCE

If you wish to contact any of the young entrepreneurs featured in this book, here are their email IDs and websites. To improve your chances of a response, be specific with your query or comment. And be a little patient!

1. **Shashank N D** – shashank@practo.com
   Abhinav Lal – abhinav@practo.com
   www.practo.com

2. **Sourabh Bansal** – sbansal@magicrete.in
   Puneet Mittal – puneetmittal@magicrete.in
   Sidharth Bansal – sidharth.bansal@magicrete.in
   www.magicrete.in

3. **Prakash Mundhra** – prakash.blessingz@gmail.com

4. **Prabhkiran Singh** – prabhkiran@bewakoof.com
   Siddharth Munot – siddharth@bewakoof.com
   www.bewakoof.com

5. **Ankit Gupta** – ankit@innovese.com
   Dhruv Sogani – dhruv@innovese.com
   Neeraj Agarwal – nee.agl@gmail.com
   www.innovese.com

6. **Rupesh Shah** – rupesh@inopen.in
   www.inopen.in

7. **Aruj Garg** – arujgarg@gmail.com

8. **Anurag Arora** – 12aarora@ibsindia.org

9. **Apurva Joshi** – apurvapj@gmail.com
   www.fraudexpress.com

10. **Eshwar Vikas** – eshwar@mukundafoods.com
    Sudeep Sabat – sudeep@mukundafoods.com
    www.dosamatic.com